OUR RESPONSES TO A DEADLY VIRUS

The Group-Analytic Approach

Angela Molnos

OUR RESPONSES
TO A DEADLY VIRUS

The Group-Analytic Approach

Angela Molnos

Published by Karnac Books
for
The Institute of Group Analysis
and The Group-Analytic Society
(London)

Karnac Books
London 1990

First published in 1990 by
H. Karnac (Books) Ltd.
58 Gloucester Road
London SW7 4QY

British Library Cataloguing in Publication Data
Molnos, Angela
  Our responses to a deadly virus
  1. Man. AIDS. Psychological aspects
  I. Title
  616.9'792'0019

ISBN 0–946439–80–X

Printed in Great Britain by BPCC Wheatons Ltd, Exeter

CONTENTS

v

ACKNOWLEDGEMENTS

For the writing of this book, I was able to use a number of reports and insightful evaluations of the experiential workshop 'Group Responses to the AIDS Crisis' sent to me by participants and staff members. I wish to extend my thanks in the first place to Sarah T. Willis for her substantial contribution. Parts of it appear in this book as independent chapters. My thanks go to the 37 people who completed the evaluation form and especially to Dr Althea de Carteret, Dr Dorothy M. Edwards, Mrs Elizabeth Foulkes, Mr John Heatley, Mr Peter La Cour, Mrs Anne Mhlongo, Mrs Brenda Roberts and Mrs Cynthia Rogers for their detailed and thoughtful accounts.

I acknowledge my indebtedness to all those who so generously shared their experience and knowledge in this field, including Dr Charles Farthing and members of his team at St Stephens Hospital, and to Mr Antony Grey, convenor of the BAC AIDS panel, who helped me to make the first contacts, to Julen Perurena as well as Kate Partridge, together with the other Health Advisers at the Praed Street Clinic, St Mary's Hospital, for contributing their observations. My thanks go to all participants of the workshop for being there and giving so much of themselves; to the members of the team who ran the workshop, the group conductors, the co-convenors and the chairman for their dedicated work and warm support.

Finally, I am grateful to Jan Adams, Janet Boakes and Beatrice Musgrave for their comments on the manuscript, as well as to Klara Majthényi King, the editor, for her untiring commitment to our shared task and, last but not least, to Cesare Sacerdoti, the publisher, for his steady encouragement.

A.M.

ABBREVIATIONS

AGIPAD   Asociación Guipuzcoana Investigación
Prevención Abuso Drogas, San Sebastian, Spain
AIDS   acquired immune deficiency syndrome
ARC   AIDS-related complex
AZT   azidothymidine or zidovudine (antiviral drug)
BAC   British Association for Counselling
BSE   bovine spongiform encephalopathy
FAIDS   feline AIDS
FTLV   feline T-lymphotropic lentivirus
GA   group analysis or group analyst
GAS   Group-Analytic Society (London)
HIV   human immunodeficiency virus: name given by
the International Committee on the Taxonomy
of Viruses, May 1986
HIV+   HIV-positive test result; also the person whose
blood test shows the antibodies indicative of the
HIV infection. It does not mean that the person
has AIDS
HIV-1   is the initial isolate, which is epidemic in
Central Africa, Haiti, Western Europe and the
United States

HIV-2   is the second subtype, more recently identified
           and found in a few West African countries such
           as Guinea-Bissau and Gambia and sporadically
           in Europe and some parts of South America
HTLV-III   human T-cell lymphotropic virus: first name
           given to HIV by the American researchers
           Popovic, M., Sarngadharan, M. G., Gallo, R. C.
           (Bethesda, Maryland) in May 1984.
IGA   Institute of Group Analysis (London)
IV   intravenous: it can mean drug users who inject
           drugs directly into their veins.
KS   Kaposi's sarcoma
LAV   lymphadenopathy-associated virus: first name
           given to HIV by the French researchers Barré-
           Sinoussi, F., Chermann, J. C., Montagnier, L.
           (Paris) in May 1983.
PCP   pneumocystis carinii pneumonia
PWA   person (people) with AIDS
SAIDS   simian AIDS
SIDA   syndrome d'immunodéficit acquis (AIDS in
           French);
           sindrome de inmunodeficiencia adquirida
           (AIDS in Spanish)
SIV   simian immunodeficiency virus
STD   sexually transmitted disease
STLV   simian T-lymphotropic virus
THT   Terrence Higgins Trust
VD   venereal disease
WHO   World Health Organization (Geneva)

PREFACE

Dr Terry E. Lear
President of the Group-Analytic Society (London)

A n English folk story tells of a stranger who finds himself isolated and fearful in an empty cottage at night. He is startled, and, as though his fright had taken on a huge form, he is pursued by it down a moonlit lane. He pauses, breathless. 'That was a good race we had', he hears, and, unwilling to take a good look at what it is beside him, in reply he says, 'Yes, and we shall have another just as soon as I catch my breath'.

There is a hint of humour in the story which could be helpful, though no human conversation nor understanding emerge to assist him, only the contemplation of his own dread.

Instead of flight, Dr Angela Molnos and the other participants sought something better through group events in a one-day workshop. Overall they found moving, worthwhile experiences and bits of understanding in the brief opportunity which they share with readers through the detailed account in the second part of this book.

The author had ideas to test. One was that the shame of having the HIV infection, or an association with such a person, or of being unable to cope with feelings of disgust and rejection, together with reactions of anger or withdrawal, could be explored by analogous experience in the quasi-laboratory situation of a workshop. It was in the so-called 'non-fishbowl' event that this idea came home to people and surprised most.

Another idea was that if the method of group-analytic psychotherapy is relevant to locate, contain and understand to some extent such feelings in experiential workshop groups, then it could have wider applications in the AIDS crisis. This proposal gained much affirmation in subsequent evaluation.

Sex talk in the groups was thought to express a longing for renewal of life as a defence against the hovering threat of death conjured by the AIDS talk. Such close encounters of participants do promise deeply satisfying intimacy between group members, which may give birth to new ideas in a safe process without physical contact or ugly consequences.

In New Orleans, a medical student showed me round the bustling floors of the Charity Hospital. I left with two impressions—one of many patients dying of AIDS, and the other a picture of rows and rows of newborn babies on the top floor.

I joined a session in a groupwork conference having AIDS as the theme. I recall a small group: among other members, the spouse of a patient, a nurse who worked in an AIDS ward, a gay therapist who, attempting to come to terms with the death of some of his AIDS patients, was concerned with burn-out, a psychiatrist who treated AIDS cases complicated by dementia, and a prison officer who reported the violent behaviour of others against prisoners with AIDS. Reading this report, I was reminded of my own experience in that New Orleans group, namely the struggle to identify the nature of my own involvement with AIDS. It wasn't the reiteration of 'everyone's involved with AIDS', but the dawning awareness that I was involved with the members of that group.

The author wrote several books based on original research in East Africa. They became textbooks for planners and policymakers in the search for a deeper understanding of social and cultural values and attitudes and their relevance to modern economic development. Among other qualifications, she is a group analyst and a social psychologist and has first-hand experience in working with those who give pre- and post-test HIV counselling and attend to AIDS patients. Despite this wealth of experience, her account reveals the courage, determination and painstaking work that was necessary to see the Workshop through. Care was the watchword—care that is, with planning, taking the context into consideration, with recruiting trained staff, with the composition of the experiential groups and with gathering after-reflections of participants for evaluation.

I am grateful to the author and participants who have assisted me to achieve more understanding by means of this account of a pioneering workshop. I believe that others, in particular those who plan similar projects, would find this book invaluable.

Northampton, England, February 1989

FOREWORD

Dr Deirdre Cunningham

Director of Public Health, Parkside Health Authority

IDS and HIV infection constitute a comparatively new public health problem, and Dr Molnos' thorough and illuminating book documents and explains many features of the responses to it. But in some respects AIDS and HIV infection merely highlight areas in which the needs of particular groups and individuals, be they patients, staff or others, have been overlooked or treated insensitively. As one who has been heavily involved in developing and evaluating health services for HIV infection in the United Kingdom, I am aware of the immense importance of looking at aspects of our services which we have previously not challenged. Unless we pay attention to staff' and patients' attitudes and perceptions, both covert and overt, we are bound to fail. Experience reported from the United States, Canada, continental Europe and the United Kingdom all indicate that whatever policies are developed and finally agreed for the delivery of health care, they always will be implemented unevenly due to differences in staff attitudes. Unless we allow and help staff to recognize, express and deal with their feelings and unless we reflect these feelings in sensitive policies, we will have ineffectual services and patients will suffer, along with the staff.

As a group analyst, Dr Molnos is unusual in that she has a particular interest in the social and psychological problems connected with HIV infection and the AIDS epidemic. After a distinguished, long and varied career in several countries, she has brought her wisdom and experience to this field. Many have written about prejudice and stigma in relation to people with AIDS, but her viewpoint is uniquely group analytic.

In the first part of the book she analyses the disturbance that HIV/AIDS causes in society and in the individual and shows how it can activate the destructive power of groups, if nothing is done to stem these effects. The logical conclusion is that group analysis should be applied to conducting staff support groups. The second part of the book is devoted to documenting experiences from a workshop the author convened in London in December 1987. Those who have talked to people with HIV infection or AIDS or their close associates or carers will recognize as familiar many of the quotations and feelings expressed.

The third and final part of the book, the synthesis, entitled 'Looking towards the future', is what the book is all about for those of us concerned with delivering effective health services. Juxtaposed with the recommendations made by participants at the experiential workshop, here we read the author's views of what group analysts have to offer. Finally, we learn about Dr Molnos' demonstrably successful application of her theory to the practice of conducting staff support groups. Her work with a group of health advisers has been extremely impressive. Its success is assessed by herself, confirmed by the participants and, what is more, can be measured also in terms which cost-conscious managers would find convincing, such as reduced staff sickness, absence and turnover and hence increased cost-effectiveness of the service. Finally, her approach has significantly contributed to reducing those boundary problems, detrimental to staff and patients, which are very evident in many areas of delivery of care to this particular group of patients.

The author's obvious interest in and insights into the issues surrounding HIV and AIDS, together with her experience in applying group-analytic principles successfully to running staff support groups, provide an introduction for the reader that will whet the appetite. This book should convince both individual carers and their managers that group analysis has much to offer and can produce tangible results. I hope that one effect of Dr Molnos' book will be to interest people in a wider application of group-analytic staff support techniques within the Health Service.

London, April 1989

THE AIDS PANDEMIC

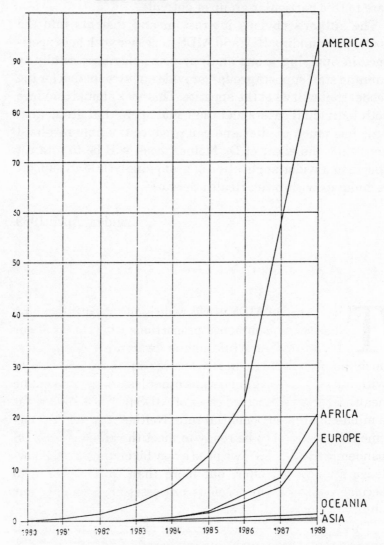

Figure 1. Number of AIDS cases in thousands reported to the World Health Organization year by year. Although these figures are low compared with other health problems, they increase steadily at an exponential rate. This trend is clearest in the Americas, where reporting approaches 90% of the presumed total. Underreporting of AIDS cases is still a problem in many other parts of the world.

INTRODUCTION

The spread of AIDS world-wide is one of the impending disasters of immense proportions that threaten our life on earth. While public awareness, like a nervously held torch, periodically focuses on it, only quickly to withdraw and cast light on some other less disturbing public health issue, the reported cases of AIDS increase steadily at a mind-boggling exponential rate. Neither a cure nor a vaccine are in sight. To be ready to meet the advancing AIDS pandemic (Koch, 1987) we need every bit of up-to-date knowledge science can offer, but more than that, we need to become aware of unconscious processes that hamper our ability to cope at all levels.

This book addresses a wide range of professionals as well as the general reader who is keen to reflect upon the ways in which our shared unconscious seems to react to the spread of the HIV infection, which is just one of the life-threatening phenomena of our age. Specifically, it has been written with the carers in mind, and for them. It intends to speak to all those who are involved in HIV/AIDS-related programmes and especially those who are in direct patient contact. Hopefully it will encourage them to explore and try to understand the nature and source of their own responses as well as those of the groups within which they work. At present those attending to HIV-positive people and AIDS patients are under great stress and often suffer psychosomatic illnesses and burn-out. Many of them abandon the field. Their invaluable expertise, gained through costly training, great personal dedication and sacrifice, is lost. New staff have to be recruited and trained.

It is also hoped that this volume will help many group analysts, psychodynamically orientated psychotherapists and counsellors to realize how much their skills are needed in this field and also prompt them to inform themselves about the virological and medical complexities of the condition called AIDS and to keep abreast with developments. That knowledge will enable them to assist and support primary care workers in their emotionally and professionally demanding work.

The global threat posed by HIV infection and AIDS becomes even more, not less, worrying when we look at the problem on the level of the individual, the group or the country. Each case of HIV infection demands the personal attention of workers from virtually every section of the caring professions: health advisers, doctors, nurses, specialist consultants—such as dermatologists, gastro-enterologists, heart and lung specialists, rheumatologists, neurologists, psychiatrists, radiotherapists—as well as nutritionists, physiotherapists, dentists, occupational therapists, social workers, home visitors, community workers, often also counsellors, psychologists, psychotherapists, priests and even those working outside the caring professions—legal advisers, the person at the dole office and so on. This list has to be extended to include the friends and relatives of the person with AIDS. Due to the complex nature of the condition and the enormous and deep anxieties connected with AIDS, the infected person requires a series of different interventions at any of the various stages and constant support far over and above normal medical care.

If all those thousands diagnosed seropositive and those who will develop AIDS in this country are to be given proper care, by the end of the century every person who works in any of the caring professions will have to be familiar with the nature of the infection, be versed in up-to-date patient management and be able to respond adequately to the social and psychological needs of those affected. This universal requirement in a civilized society will put a tremendous emotional stress on hundreds of thousands of carers. Millions of us will be affected one way or the other by what has been aptly termed the 'ultimate challenge' (Kübler-Ross, 1987).

* * *

At the core of this book are the participants who attended the workshop 'Group Responses to the AIDS Crisis' on 5 December 1987. The sum total of their personal and professional experiences, their practical and scientific knowledge covers all the treacherous intricacies of the HIV/AIDS field. Together they stand for all those who in ever-growing numbers care for patients living with AIDS and dying from it, for health advisers and others who do pre-test counselling, help HIV-positive persons and give care to people with AIDS, for doctors who find it hard to admit to emotional stress and for administrators and managers of HIV/AIDS-related programmes. This book is not just about one workshop, but about the extreme anxieties, emotions and wild associations AIDS generates in groups and the mental and institutional confusion it causes. The one-day workshop at the Institute of Group Analysis may be viewed both as holding a mirror to the above processes and as a possible example to follow.

In writing this book, I also hoped to make a contribution to the group-analytic understanding of the phenomena that have surrounded the threat of AIDS in this country up to the end of the 1980s and might continue recurring under the same or similar conditions of collective anxiety.

* * *

I divided this book into three parts:

The first part sets out the wider frame of reference—the various aspects of the AIDS epidemic, the nature of the HIV infection, how it affects individuals and groups. Group analysis, its essence and its relevance to dealing with HIV/ AIDS-related problems are introduced.

The second part of this volume, which has been brought into focus in the Preface, attempts to convey the workshop participants' very personal, yet universal responses to HIV/ AIDS. It also describes in detail the preparations and mechanics of the workshop, together with its step-by-step evaluation.

The third part, which has been emphasized in the Foreword, points to the future. The application of group-analytic principles, especially to conducting staff support groups for carers of AIDS patients and those who do HIV test counselling, is discussed and documented. A chapter on 'Strange phenomena' gives concrete examples of the confusion created by HIV/AIDS and also illustrates how in the future collective anxieties might move from AIDS towards other areas.

There are two illustrations in the book. Figure 1, entitled 'The AIDS Pandemic', highlights the magnitude of the potential threat; figure 2, at the end of the text, symbolizes the small group conducted along group-analytic lines as the place where overstressed carers can share their anxieties and find deep understanding, tolerance and support.

This book contains a variety of material: not only factual accounts and overviews, theoretical expositions by myself and reports of my own personal experiences, but also analyses, summaries of specialist addresses and workshop sessions by various contributors, working documents and so on. The distinct styles have been maintained deliberately, and it is hoped that the resulting variety of modes and tones, with the frequent shifts of focus from the general to the particular, will be stimulating for the reader.

For the sake of consistency and in order to avoid the clumsy repetition of 'he/she', 'she' is used throughout the text when referring to the conductor of a group and 'he' when referring to a group member. The pronoun 'he' is also used for a person affected by HIV, ARC or AIDS. The reader will bear in mind that persons of either sex can be infected.

London, April 1989

PART ONE

The psychological and social impact of a virus

CHAPTER ONE

The reversal of meanings, values and attitudes

> . . . the peril which threatens all of us comes not
> from nature, but from man, from the psyches of the
> individual and the mass.
>
> [C.G. Jung, 1961]

The sinister features
of the retrovirus called HIV

Science responded quickly to the threat posed by AIDS to our existence. Within two years—from mid-1982 to mid-1984—the hitherto unknown human immunodeficiency virus (HIV) was isolated, its way of operating within the body by and large clarified, a blood test devised and the foreseeable extent of the epidemic assessed. Since then progress has been slower: '. . . in some respects the virus has outpaced science. No cure or vaccine is yet available, and the epidemic continues to spread.' (Gallo and Montagnier, 1988, p. 25).

9

As this book goes to press, AIDS is still an incurable condition. Its lethal course can be delayed by highly skilled and dedicated medical care, but it cannot be altered. The fiendish nature of the retrovirus that causes AIDS is such that scientists are unable even to forecast the time when a preventative vaccine will be found, let alone a cure. HIV is deceptive on more than one account. Its extreme smallness enables it, if it so chooses, to slip through the blood/brain barrier and play havoc in the mind before any other physical damage occurs. It also taxes the scientists' minds by being an elusively fast-mutating virus. Assuming that a vaccine is found, its effectiveness could be short-lived if new forms of HIV continue to appear.

The retrovirus HIV lodges itself within the very cells on which we rely for protection against the invasion of germs. HIV is the enemy who, undetected, manages to infiltrate our defence system. It can remain dormant for even a decade and more before deciding to launch its attack from within the well-organized fortress of an apparently healthy organism. The mortal onslaught starts from within as the immune system goes into action to fend off a minor infection. AIDS, the acquired immune deficiency syndrome, resulting from the HIV infection, is the ultimate symbol of our vulnerability. It is the invisible illness that cannot be described because it is nothing but the unexpected incapability of the infected body to react against other illnesses.

What interests us here is that the retrovirus called HIV goes beyond the physical destruction of individual bodies. It does so in several ways. The closeness to its simian (STLV/SIV/SAIDS) and other animal counterparts (FTLV/FAIDS etc.) can strike one as rather unnerving. Also, the psychological impact of HIV on groups and individuals seems to be linked mysteriously with its uncanny, even sinister physical features. Its insidious ways of operating conjure up thoughts of archetypal Evil. It affects virtually all aspects of civilized life, breaking taboos at an unprecedented rate, leading to the rapid reversal of cherished values, traditional and progressive alike, and opening the flood-gates to images of chaos and terror.

The language around HIV/AIDS
and semantic distortions

Our language is being affected by AIDS. In English, we lost an elegant synonym of 'helps' (Burgess, 1987). The identical sound of the acronym 'AIDS' and the verb 'aids' mocks us in the same bewildering fashion as the retrovirus that manages to integrate itself into the genetic structure of the very cells that nature designed to save us from danger.

We are also engaged in an ongoing ritual of linguistic avoidance dances to boost the morale or at least to spare the sensitivities of groups most directly under pressure in the AIDS crisis. These rituals involve mainly prohibitions and restrictions on our usage of the language. They lead to semantic losses and sad deformations. None of these rituals creates beauty.

The concept 'positive', for instance, has suffered several reversals in the AIDS crisis. First, its meaning was reversed when it acquired the ominous connotation stuck in the ears of the person who has had the HIV test and has been told that he is HIV positive or seropositive. Then an attempt to re-reverse it was made with the expression 'body positive'—an invocation to fight, not to give in, to take care of the HIV-infected body by adopting an active, assertive, optimistic attitude.

Semantically speaking, it is correct to say that someone suffers from headaches or is the victim of a car accident or a serious illness. Not so with AIDS. One cannot say 'AIDS sufferer' or 'AIDS victim' without provoking considerable irritation among those who have contracted the condition and those who care for them and identify with them. 'Sufferer' or 'victim' imply acceptance, passive endurance and therefore—so the false inference goes—pity and condescension on the part of the speaker. The ideology around HIV/AIDS is that if you are infected, you have to try to live life as normally as possible. You must remain determined to be normal. You must refuse to be a 'victim' or even a 'sufferer'. You can be a PWA. Thus, our language is defiled by the forced penetration of yet another ugly acronym. It would be a small price to pay if it helped those who suffer. However, waging battle on the terrain of semantics might be just a displacement activity that offers relief only for an instant. AIDSpeak has developed in order to avoid troublesome expressions that might offend and to '. . . make everyone content. AIDSpeak was the language of good intentions in the AIDS epidemic; AIDSpeak was the language of death' (Shilts, 1988, p. 315).

'Living with AIDS' is the war-cry; fighting it is mandatory. The language of AIDS is full of the terminology of war. In the debate after a lecture on the spread of AIDS, the chairman apologized to a discussant for not having noticed that he was a 'frontliner'. The implication was that as a 'frontliner', special respect and precedence over the other discussants was due to him. The meaning of 'frontliner' is that the person not only is infected with HIV, but also has full-blown AIDS. He fights alongside others against all odds, determined not to surrender to the enemy. The tone of the apology clearly indicated that the chairman, a world-famous, but noninfected AIDS specialist, felt less of a hero, and somehow less credible than the 'frontliner' who had no medical qualifications. It is inherent in the vocabulary of war that one fights to win. In the battle against AIDS, those who fight can only win time. It is possible to overthrow this statement by saying that we are all doing precisely that, whether or not we are infected. The name of the fatal illness is life itself. It is invariably followed by death. Nevertheless, from a semantic point of view the conventional pre-AIDS meaning of 'frontliner'—that of the champion, the physically strong man in the front rank—has changed.

Under the influence of the reality to which we repeatedly apply words and expressions their connotations are modified. If we were consistently to describe people who are close to death as being still 'alive', after a time the word 'alive' itself would acquire a deadly resonance. The new meaning of 'frontliner' still carries the ancient images of a vanguard of muscular men spearheading the battle. However, that vision is clouded now by precisely those connotations AIDSpeak intends to eradicate: the images of emaciated figures with no strength left, glazed looks or a last charming smile, suffering, waiting for death to come.

Values and attitudes

Sex, love, life and blood

Worse than the invasion of our language, and hand in hand with it, goes the sudden assault on values and attitudes that were taken for granted before HIV/AIDS appeared on the TV screen and in the press. Liberal, progressive attitudes towards sex are being reversed because of fear and not because of a newly found morality. Often the necessity to protect oneself from HIV infection is confusingly equated with an alleged rediscovery of puritanical values concerning sex. On the other hand, explicit sex talk has become dull and commonplace. Not even in the permissive 1960s could condoms be discussed and their proper use visually illustrated on the screen, as they are now. Reciprocal masturbation is being publicized as a commendable alternative to unprotected intercourse. Everyone has to be thoroughly informed, and there is no room for prudery, shyness or ingrained sensitivities and traditional good taste. Terms and expressions like anal sex, blow-job, rimming and fisting are used publicly. You have to be overexplicit to make sure that the message comes across. . . .

The reversal of values goes deeper than questions of sexual 'morality', abstinence, monogamy or promiscuity (with or without safe sex). Whether we are at risk or not at all, the very essence of love-making has been affected. Forbidden, restricted or free for all, by and large it used to be pleasure and fun. The sexually transmitted diseases of the past, gonorrhoea and syphilis, had become curable in this century. Even an unwanted pregnancy—the only major risk connected with love-making before AIDS—could give way to a more or less enjoyable new life. Over the last years, AIDS has crept into the intimacy of bedrooms, introducing an ominous association between life-generating encounter, sweet physical closeness and death. Love-making used to be the privileged domain of the young, nostalgically envied by the old. Not so since love-making can lead to HIV infection, AIDS and death. Today, the old are in a more enviable position.

No matter which way we look at it, physically or symbolically, the human immunodeficiency virus is a direct attack on life itself, at its very core. The transmission occurs principally via blood, semen and vaginal fluid. Other bodily fluids, like the saliva, contain far too low a concentration of the virus to be dangerous. Both blood and semen signify life and potential life in a concrete way. Blood is also the symbol of the libido itself, of feeling alive, passionate, being inextricably connected—as in blood brotherhood, blood pact or actually being someone's blood relation. Blood is between the body and the spirit, the mediator between Christ and his followers, the way to eternal life in the communion. It can be abused by vampires, black magic, the mentally deranged and the criminal, but in itself it remains the symbol of life. That is, until the advent of AIDS. Now, HIV-infected blood becomes anti-life. A syringeful of it can be used as a lethal weapon to threaten anyone.

The reversal of values affects our institutions, among them the Church itself, causing chaos in official attitudes. The silent acknowledgement that not all members of the Anglican and Catholic clergy were able to follow the sexual mores prescribed by their respective Churches is now painfully in the open. A newspaper article talks about a priest dying of AIDS in the States. On the whole, the modern

Churches demonstrate a deeply caring and loving attitude towards the sick and dying, including those affected by AIDS. The real conflict starts when the sufferer is a fellow clergyman. The conflict is agonizing. The homosexual HIV-infected clergyman has not only broken his promise of fidelity to the Church, but he is also guilty of deception. He betrayed the trust of his congregation. Abuse and scorn is thrown at the Church because of him. Those whom we so much need now, the spiritual leaders of the past, are forced into defensive corners. No wonder that one hears relatively few apocalyptic pronouncements about the sins of the world and the well-deserved devastation of this Sodom and Gomorrah. There is a feeling of impending apocalypse around AIDS, but except for the sensation-seeking press, no spiritual leader dares to make the link.

Prejudice and counter-prejudice

AIDS is also an assault on our social values and decency. One of the most cherished moral principles is that the strong should refrain from crushing the weak, the majority should not oppress or impose on the minority, and that we ought to be able to tolerate our differences. The appearance of AIDS works against these principles. It strengthens the position of those who want to exert their power over the weak or numerically inferior and provokes corresponding counter-reactions in those who feel oppressed. Sadly enough, HIV/AIDS creates a fertile environment in which old and new prejudices and counter-prejudices can thrive and groups grow apart in increasing reciprocal intolerance. The fact that in Britain and in Europe as a whole HIV infection is still more prevalent among practising homosexuals than heterosexuals fuels anti-gay attitudes as well as powerful counter-prejudices against the 'persecuting' and 'oppressive' heterosexual majority. Homosexual men with AIDS are at times treated more hurtfully than lepers. Others, who are neither HIV positive nor homosexual, can also be hurt again and again when their offer to help is dismissed by the minority.

Uncannily and consistently selective, AIDS attacks sensitivities and provokes the anger of already marginalized minorities who might respond with furious outrage. A glaring example of a new counter-prejudice was produced by a black activist saying that it was a deliberate and malicious slander on the part of white man to suggest that the virus originated in Africa. AIDS feeds into most of our prejudices and counter-prejudices: against the Government, for not allocating enough resources to AIDS programmes or for giving it far too high a priority, for not doing enough to increase public awareness of the epidemic or for creating panic with too much publicity; against the 'cold', 'unfeeling' legal profession, insurance brokers and mortgage lenders who deny the rights of those who are HIV positive; against the 'vociferous', 'demanding' minority who refuses even to consider the global economic point of view and the interests of the non-infected citizens.

Prejudices against the inmates of prisons, where HIV infection is rampant, against intravenous drug-users and their lifestyles, are being powerfully reinforced. Intravenous drug-users have become the second-largest group infected in the UK. Any talk about 'innocent victims'—babies born with the HIV infection transmitted from the mother and haemophiliacs who received HIV-infected blood transfusions—is just a convenient device to condemn the rest with licence. 'The staff would not have gone near him had he not been a haemophiliac. As it was, everyone's heart went out to him; he was so young and completely innocent.' This is how a colleague of mine spoke about the first AIDS patient they had in the local hospital in a small town in the north of the country in mid-1986. Among those who care for HIV-infected haemophiliacs, a particular kind of bitterness and anger prevails. Sometimes there is a tendency to close ranks and exclude those who care for the less 'innocent' victims of the epidemic.

The spread of AIDS in Africa through prostitution makes it more difficult to feel warmth and compassion towards the girl pacing the streets of Nairobi. She has to maintain herself and her dependents living in a far-away rural area. She has no other way to survive and to discharge her traditional obligations to her family than to catch the lethal virus, transmit it to others and ultimately to die from its consequences herself. Our attitudes towards prostitution are bound to harden, and we will end up by disregarding her predicament. And what about our horror and hatred of the pimp, the drug-pusher and the drug-trafficker, the most effective agents of HIV worldwide? What is left of Christian forgiveness to extend to them? Have not I, as a Christian, been taught to forgive all sinners? Furthermore, what are we supposed to feel if we heed the suggestion that terrorist bombs and hijackings are mainly financed with money laundered from drug-trafficking? Is not then the circle of prejudice, counter-prejudice and reciprocal intolerance made complete and consolidated into an inescapable nightmare that affects all our lives and thinking?

CHAPTER TWO

Anxieties and emotions of individuals affected by HIV/ARC/AIDS

Observations by J. Perurena

The following is an adapted and shortened version of a paper by Julen Perurena Lizarazu, a psychologist, working at AGIPAD, San Sebastián, Spain, entitled 'Aspectos psicológicos de los portadores del VIH, CRS y SIDA'. The author's experience derives mainly from counselling and treating HIV-positive drug addicts in groups and individually as well as inpatients of both sexes in hospitals throughout the various stages of ARC and AIDS. The AIDS-related complex, or ARC, is the last stage in the progression of HIV infection before full-blown AIDS develops and is characterized by particularly debilitating symptoms. However, it has to be pointed out that not all AIDS patients go through ARC.

Although the psycho-social background to this contribution is specific to Northern Spain, the author's observations might enable those who have no first-hand experience of such patients to imagine the massive anxieties and emotional reactions facing primary care workers, counsellors and psychologists in HIV/AIDS-related programmes anywhere in the world.

G iven the ways and the social contexts in which HIV infection, ARC and full-blown AIDS prevalently occur and the fact that a medical solution has yet to be found, for the time being we have no choice but to adopt a combined multidisciplinary approach, applying social, psychological and medical knowledge and experience.

In the following, we want to focus on the psychological reactions that appear from the moment a person decides to have the HIV test while he is still free from physical symptoms and is given an HIV-positive result, up to the time when he develops ARC/AIDS and finally dies. Although each individual is unique and the responses to the same situation differ from one person to the other, an attempt will be made to pinpoint the most frequently observed responses.

Before the HIV test result

In most cases, there is an internal struggle before someone decides to have the test. To go for the test means to face a fear that may be justified. Many things will depend on the result of the test. If it is confirmed that the fear was well founded, nothing will ever be the same again.

In the period preceding the test, the question, 'Do I have the virus in my body or not?' is likely to be accompanied by various emotions, changes of mood, irritability, agitation, intense fear, obsessive thoughts, preoccupation with physical symptoms, difficulty in concentrating, depression. Such emotional turmoil can engender psychosomatic disturbances. Physical symptoms such as digestive troubles, lack of appetite, weight loss, diarrhoea, sleeplessness, headaches and muscular pain can stem from merely psychic sources.

The psychotherapeutic objective is to contain the great anxiety, and pre-test counselling is a must. Accurate information and interventions designed to diminish the intense fear are its most important aspects.

HIV-positive test result

Invariably, the person who is told that he is seropositive will have a strong emotional reaction. It can present itself in many forms, from shock, through anger, to tears. The intensity of the reaction will depend on how well or little the person is informed, the personality characteristics and the situation in which the person finds himself within the social context.

It is important to remember what HIV infection means and implies:

since the transmission occurs through behaviours that go against prevalent social norms, a likelihood of being subjected to recriminations and social rejection;

a requirement for preventative measures against infections for the rest of the person's life;

the likelihood of a terminal condition, i.e. AIDS;

all relationships between the HIV-infected person and others are altered and adversely affected by concomitant anxieties.

Let us reiterate that nothing is the same as before. The HIV-positive person has the hard task of having to cope with fierce and sometimes contradictory emotional reactions within himself. His own death is suddenly present and all-pervasive. From the moment he knows he is carrying the virus, which might be activated at any unforeseeable time, the thought of death appears, constantly recurs and might become obsessive. The main emotional components of this internal stress situation are anxiety, anguish, feelings of impotence and insecurity. There might be the magical wish to put the clock back in time: 'If only I could undo the past and start again.'

During this period up to the appearance of the first symptoms, the HIV-positive person experiences intense emotions

that alternate between opposites in a manic-depressive fashion or are mingled together, causing enormous psychic pain.
One set of feelings and thoughts represents a flight from
reality or an attempt to get rid of the problem by placing it
somehow outside himself. The opposite tendency is to turn it
on himself.

> Externalization: 'I'll beat this'. . . 'I am paying for other
> people's sins'. . . looking for whoever might be responsible
> . . . destructive wishes towards others . . . unrealistic plans.

> Internalization: self-accusations: 'There is nothing I can
> do' . . . 'I brought it upon myself'—self-directed hatred
> . . . gloom and resignation: 'There is no future for me.'

This strong intrapsychic conflict between contradictory
impulses, emotions, feelings and thoughts is further exacer-
bated in relationships as a result of the anxieties being HIV
positive provokes in others. The fear of being reproached,
rejected and socially isolated is added to the fear about the
person's physical condition. There is a need to revise his
situation within relationships and social life in the light of
the risk of infecting others and the uncertainty of the future.

Summing up, people who have been diagnosed HIV positive but have not yet developed ARC or AIDS are likely to
respond with depression, social withdrawal and suicidal
thoughts as a way of evading intolerable tension and anxiety, as well as psychosomatic disturbances and a strong
preoccupation with any alteration in their physical well-
being. The intensity of these reactions and the extent to
which they, in their turn, will have further negative reper-
cussions depend on the person's background, personality
characteristics, how his life is organized and on what social
support he is able to rely. The psychotherapeutic objective in
this period has to be the patient's practical re-orientation
and emotional containment.

The appearance of ARC

With the help of good post-test counselling, the knowledge of being seropositive allows the person to begin to come to terms with the much-feared condition before it manifests itself. Nevertheless, the appearance of the first symptoms has a strong psychological impact. The previous fears are now founded on concrete physical conditions. Moreover, the patient enters a phase during which his body is submitted to the multiple onslaught of infections, tests and treatments. All this causes physical and emotional exhaustion. Each new symptom or the repetition of the previous one causes psychological stress, which can then be compounded by the secondary effects of medication.

This is a period of confusion and dejection in which the fear of physical pain and suffering appears. The prominent psychological condition is depression, and it is important to distinguish between the two main forms it can take. The symptoms of the depression due to having developed ARC are mostly tiredness, loss of weight and sleeplessness. By contrast, the symptoms characteristic of deep depression, which is rooted in underlying problems preceding the appearance of ARC, include confusion, difficulty in making decisions, feelings of failure and being punished, frequent crying, loss of interest for others and suicidal thoughts. The differential criterion is low self-esteem in deep depression. To treat it, one has to take into account earlier depressive episodes and suicide attempts.

In this phase, previous intrapsychic conflicts are bound to recur. There is a regression of the oral type with a strong need for attention. Suicidal thoughts are common, and their verbal expression has to be taken as a cry for help. The psychological symptoms typical of the HIV-positive person are present, but they are aggravated by the physical evidence of the condition, which can no longer be concealed from himself or others—the family, the partner, friends, the whole social environment. His condition becomes an obsession. A patient described it like this: 'I have lost one and a half stone in a week and I cannot eat. The doctors don't tell me whether or not this is AIDS. I've had enough. If I put on the TV, there is AIDS. If I pick up the newspaper, I see AIDS. I have great difficulty in getting some sleep. My girl wants me to tell her what I have, but I don't know. . . . When the word AIDS comes to my mind I cannot cope with it.' The defence mechanism of denial may also be in operation, minimizing the seriousness of the condition, distorting reality and allowing the patient to make unrealistic plans for the future (e.g., start to study at university, establish a family). As infections appear and intermittently disappear following treatment and new symptoms develop—which, in their turn, are treated, with more or less success—there is a certain measure of habituation to the less severe symptoms (temperatures, diarrhoea, etc.) and all that goes with the condition (readmission to hospital, medications, etc.). In many patients the panic is stronger at the first symptoms than when the same symptoms recur or new ones present themselves.

As mentioned, the appearance of first symptoms has a traumatic impact, but having anticipated them softens the blow somewhat. Learning that he is HIV positive after the first ARC or AIDS symptoms have appeared is a far greater shock for the patient. The emotional and behavioural reactions are similar, but more intense and dramatic. This is a predicament that requires a careful approach to the individual and his particular situation on the part of the professionals who treat him. The objectives are to contain, guide and support the patient.

Diagnosis: AIDS

On the whole, patients do not notice or experience the passage from ARC to AIDS. As the difference is masked by the effects of medications, the advance of the condition bypasses their awareness.

At a certain stage the patient has infections that neither remit nor respond to treatment. Often patients describe the experience by saying: 'I have something here inside that is eating me and killing me little by little.' There is a great fear of physical pain. The emotional reactions can range from profound anguish, demands for attention, swift changes of mood, irritability, complaints, whimsical behaviour to complete apathy. It is a stage of considerable psychic pain.

The patient faces the task of having to 'repair' his relationship with significant persons in his life, to heal rifts often aggravated by his having contracted HIV. Whether he will be able to regain his self-esteem will depend on their acceptance of him and his condition, alongside mutual forgiveness and reconciliation. There is also the need to say good-bye to friends and acquaintances. Finally, there are mundane issues to be dealt with as well, such as making a will. In many cases religious faith emerges as a way of not losing hope.

In this phase, it is important to maintain physical comfort and to ensure that the patient does not feel rejected or isolated socially or emotionally. The AIDS patient might feel rejected when he senses that the attitude or behaviour of someone close to him has subtly changed.

It is important to adapt the approach to the individual's personality. While alleviating the physical pain through medication, there is a need to offer unconditional support and to make one's genuine interest in the person and his predicament felt. The objective is to accompany the person through a painful process of loss and grief.

CHAPTER THREE

The relevance
of group analysis

Perhaps the most important contribution which
this technique will make is to a social psychopathology.

[Foulkes, 1964, p. 99]

The AIDS crisis and group analysis

In the previous chapters it was attempted to show the all-pervasive disturbance HIV/AIDS causes in society at large on the one hand and in the individual who is directly affected on the other. Both society as a whole and the isolated individual are abstractions. Between them there is the human reality of myriads of interlocking groups with their declared objectives and hidden agenda, variety of structures, sizes, stability and duration. The location of the disturbance has to be found in the groups to which the individual belongs and of which society is composed. In the passage quoted at the beginning of chapter 1, C. G. Jung used the term 'mass'. Now, nearly three decades later, it should read 'group'.

We have to consider the total situation in which people with HIV infection, their partners and families find themselves. This includes their access to relevant information at appropriate intellectual and emotional levels, the social and economic conditions in which they live, housing, the distance they have to travel for treatment, means of transport, moral and material support at home and so on. As the treatment of PWAs becomes more sophisticated, all this is increasingly taken into account by medical personnel, hospital and home support teams, health advisers, social workers and other professionals. What is often left out for all practical purposes is the situation of the carers themselves and the managers of HIV/AIDS-related programmes.

Group-analytic theory offers a frame of reference that helps to understand via the group the link between the individual and society at large. It provides us with an in-depth view of the psychic mechanisms—especially denial, splitting and projection—in operation as a defence against fear and irrational rage. Group analysis can pinpoint the unconscious interactions between individuals, within the numerous groups involved in HIV/AIDS programmes and between these groups. It makes the destructive power of groups more comprehensible and enables us to find the best points of intervention in order to activate and strengthen the healing power that groups equally possess.

The principles and experience gained from the practice of group-analytic psychotherapy can be applied to help any type of group and its members to function better with each other, within themselves and with other groups. In practice, group analysis has taught us to look at the total situation and to see the individual, suffering from mental anguish or from a physical condition, within his social network. It has also taught us to pay painstaking attention to detail if we want to understand, and before we presume that we can change for the better, the total situation in a group or institution. To understand the individual, we look at the group. To understand the group, we look at the nitty-gritty of the interactions between the individuals in it, at their communications at conscious and, above all, at unconscious levels. The application to the AIDS crisis is clear. For those readers who are not familiar with group analysis, a brief outline of its essence follows.

Theoretical assumptions

Group analysis has grown from the same ground as psychoanalysis to become a completely independent method in its own right. Its founder, S. H. Foulkes, a well-known psychoanalyst who had studied and worked in Vienna and Frankfurt between the two World Wars, came to London in 1933. In his words, 'Group analysis is a form of psychotherapy in small groups and also a method of studying groups and the behaviour of human individuals in their social aspects' (Foulkes, 1948, Preface).

The three major theoretical sources to which group analysis is linked are: psychoanalysis, Gestalt theory and Foulkes' strongly held view of the social nature of man.

Group analysis incorporates psychoanalytic theory and, more specifically, such premises as the existence and dynamics of the unconscious mind and the concomitant psychic mechanisms and phenomena: repression, defences, intrapsychic conflicts, regression, repetition compulsion, transference, countertransference and so on. Foulkes also accepts the tripartite mental structure of ego, id and superego postulated by Freud.

In contrast with psychoanalysis, which focuses on the individual's internal processes, group-analytic theory revolves around the group as a totality. The idea of the group as a whole is consistent with the tenets of Gestalt theory, which was the other important conceptual frame of reference for the founder of group analysis.

When he describes the group as a whole not as a theoretical construct, but as a reality, Foulkes adheres to the principles and uses the phraseology of Gestalt theory: 'what we experience in the first place is the *group as a whole*' (Foulkes, 1957, p. 26) and 'the function of the group as a whole has . . . a more primary significance for the understanding of all part processes concerning its members, and not the other way round ("trans-personal processes")' (ibid., p. 19). Fundamentally, 'any situation in which we operate decides all the part-processes which we observe' (Foulkes, 1972, p. 1) and 'the whole is prior and more elementary than its parts' (Foulkes, 1957, p. 20). Hence the group is not a sum of its members, but a totality.

Most importantly, Foulkes had an uncompromisingly clear and consistent view of man's social nature. This view constitutes the unifying force behind group-analytic theory.

'What stands in need of explanation is not the existence of groups but *the existence of individuals*' (ibid., 234–235). This statement, perhaps more than any other, reveals how radical Foulkes' view is about man's social nature. It is not the result of a later 'additional conditioning "outside" influence' (Foulkes, 1948, p. 15), but, on the contrary, it is 'an irreducible basic fact' (Foulkes, 1964, p. 109). The social aspect is essential and not just peripheral to human nature (Foulkes, 1957, p. 234; 1964, p. 109), so much so that there is a social or interpersonal unconscious (Foulkes, 1957, pp. 42 and 56; 1964, pp. 52 and 296) that precedes the emergence of the individual consciousness (Foulkes, 1964, p. 258).

The fundamental nature of human interrelatedness means that psychic development, as well as psychic disturbances and their treatment, only takes place within a network of relationships. All mental processes are 'multi-personal events' (Foulkes, 1972, p. 29), all psychopathology, psychology, psychotherapy is social, 'based on intra-psychic processes in their interaction.' (Foulkes, 1957, p. 30).

The practice of group-analytic psychotherapy

Although the above outlined theoretical principles are consistent with and can be corroborated in the practice of group-
analytic psychotherapy, the latter was not deduced from a
priori tenets, but it developed through an empirical process
of observation, discovery, continuous search and systematic
validation. Foulkes set aside any preconceived ideas in order
to study the group situation and group phenomena. His
maxim was: 'Keep free to develop such concepts as are born
out of the group situation and relevant to it!' (1964, p. 121). In
fact, as a psychotherapeutic method group analysis started
in Foulkes' private psychoanalytic practice and out-patient
clinics in 1940 (ibid., p. 38). He had observed that haphazard
groups of patients in the waiting room were able to talk
freely and constructively to each other. Their communications seemed to have layers of conscious and unconscious
meanings.

Group-analytic psychotherapy and psychoanalysis share
the same objective, that is, to achieve fundamental changes
in the individual. The whole group-analytic technique is
geared towards this end. The therapeutic change occurs in
the group, through the group and by the group. Therefore,
the group-analytic approach implies that the ultimate objective—the fundamental change in the individual—can only
be attained by establishing the group as a whole and maintaining it from session to session. We can call this the intermediate objective. Finally, in order to form and sustain the
group as a whole, we have to make sure that nothing important is swept under the carpet, that in each session the group
unconscious is made conscious, at least in the mind of its
conductor. This is the immediate objective of which the group
conductor is aware all the time.

The conductor sets up the analytic group by selecting its
members and by establishing its boundaries. The selection
criteria (Foulkes, 1975, p. 70) are geared to create a group
powerfully capable to activate itself (Molnos, 1979) or, in

other words, to establish, strengthen and mobilize the group unconscious. Although an analytic group is an artificially created quasi-laboratory situation in which total strangers come together, a shared unconscious quickly develops. This phenomenon should not strike us as surprising. Phylogenetically, culturally and ontogenetically the social unconscious precedes the emergence of individual consciousness. Members of an analytic group have a lot in common even before they meet, no matter how heterogeneous their disturbances are.

The constancy of the boundaries of time, space and conduct required make the group 'safe' against intrusion from outside and destruction from inside. They also counteract the development of any permanent internal structure. For instance, in order to prevent sub-group formations, members are required not to meet outside the group. Consistent boundaries and the internal structural fluidity together facilitate the activation of the group unconscious and the possibility of bringing disturbances to the light of consciousness.

If we look at what is not psychoanalytic in group analysis, we might find that all the differences can be retraced to the one central difference—namely, that group analysis deals principally with the group unconscious while psychoanalysis deals with the individual unconscious. While all psychoanalytical concepts, clinical and theoretical, are 'firmly rooted ... in the one- and later in the two-personal situation' (Foulkes, 1957, p. 17), group analysis is equally firmly rooted in the multi-person situation and ultimately in the reality of the group unconscious.

The 'free associations' of psychoanalysis are replaced by 'group associations' in the so-called 'free-floating group discussion'. The group members' responses to each other's contributions are being treated as associations to a common context, as based on the unconscious as well as conscious understanding of each other. We accept that ideas and comments expressed by different members have the value of unconscious interpretations (Foulkes, 1957, pp. 28–29). As a consequence there is less need for the group conductor to interpret than a psychoanalyst does. The bulk of the work is done by the group.

Unlike in psychoanalysis, where the here-and-now transference is constantly being linked to the past, group-analytical uncovering work can be done on material in the immediate present. There is less need to recall the past, to deal with it by going back to earlier stages of individual libidinal development. The individual members' past is continually present and being worked through in the intense here-and-now experience of multiple therapeutic relationships. The fluid, unstructured group situation allows each participant to re-live in it any number and shape of relationships from his past. It facilitates an emotional and communicative re-enactment of the past in the present.

The other important difference is that the conductor becomes more real than the traditional 'blank screen' psychoanalyst. Although neither of them makes personal disclosures, more of the group analyst becomes visible as he is seen interacting with a number of different individuals and responding to a great variety of multi-personal situations. Consequently, transference neurosis is less likely to develop to a full extent than in individual psychoanalysis. Finally, if 'mirror reactions' help to differentiate the self from the not-self in individual psychoanalysis, as in the development of a baby, this process of gaining a sharper self-consciousness and of overcoming narcissism is intensified in the 'hall of mirrors' of the group situation (Foulkes, 1957, pp. 150–151).

Having looked at these major characteristics that distinguish group-analytic psychotherapy from individual psychoanalysis, it is important to point out some of the many similarities and parallels as well: steady and firm boundaries; 'suspended action'; abstinence; lack of set tasks; potential freedom for the patient to be entirely himself; tolerance and non-judgemental acceptance of all communications on the part of the analyst; profound respect for the patient's true feelings; on the patient's side, anxiety about the conflict between opposing impulses and, if the therapeutic work is successful, expression of the true feelings in the here-and-now and the emotional–cognitive recognition of the links with current and past experiences.

This set of characteristics common to psychoanalytic and group-analytic practice helps to differentiate the latter from other non-analytic, or only partly analytic, group psychotherapies and group work (e.g., drama therapy, art therapy in groups, transactional analysis in groups, gestalt techniques in groups, marathon groups).

Abstaining from activities other than verbal communications creates suspended action, distinctive of the analytic approach, and has the objective of maintaining a sufficiently high level of anxiety to mobilize the collective unconscious of the group, to bring the true feelings to the surface in the here-and-now and to facilitate their verbal expression.

The psychotherapeutic process takes place on many levels of consciousness at the same time. For clarity's sake one can single out the two major axes of the process—the emotional and the cognitive. Neither mere emotional experience (i.e., catharsis) nor mere head-level understanding (i.e., intellectual insight) bring about lasting therapeutic change.

The ever-changing analytic group acts as a projection field for as many different families as the number of its members. However, it does not react as the original families did. With its growing culture of openness, honesty, compassion and reciprocal tolerance, it offers a new constructive outcome to the old conflicts, a 'corrective emotional experience' (Alexander & French, 1980, pp. 66, 338). This time the 'family' understands, accepts the child and helps it to grow up.

Application to staff support groups

Conducting staff support groups is one of the obvious applications of group analysis. A clarity of purpose should be the starting point. While group-analytic psychotherapy is geared towards achieving fundamental changes in the group members, the ultimate aim of a staff support group is more limited—to help its members to function better at work. The likely personal benefits can be regarded as an added bonus.

The adaptation consists in focusing on the group's specific problems while adhering to all other group-analytic principles. The conductor's work is geared towards activating the healing forces intrinsic in all groups, by clarifying and protecting the boundaries and fostering a climate of honesty, reciprocal acceptance and tolerance. Apart from having more limited goals and an agreed or declared task, in all other respects staff support groups can function as group-analytic therapy groups do.

The unobtrusive, yet firm leadership of group analysts as conductors of staff support groups is a useful role-model that can have beneficial effects on how primary care workers will in their turn run other groups. Above all, the clear boundaries of time, space and conduct required (Molnos, 1979, 1987), which characterize groups conducted along analytic lines, should provide the example and first-hand experience that primary care workers badly need to protect themselves against excessive demands and pressures in their jobs and from the institutional chaos that often threatens to engulf them. The question of staff support groups will be further discussed in chapter 15.

CHAPTER FOUR

Healing power
and destructive power
of groups

*The following is the text of the talk I delivered under the title,
'Healing power and destructive power of groups' in the workshop presented in Part 2 of this book. The aim of the talk was to
outline my observations and personal experiences as honestly
as possible in the hope that participants would be encouraged
by it to do likewise in the subsequent group discussions.*

Mr Chairman, friends: apart from a few exceptions, we know each other either personally or
through the telephone or per correspondence.
Since the day the Committee of the Group-Analytic Society
gave the go-ahead for this workshop, and especially over the
last months, I have been thinking a lot about this moment
with all of us here, today.

The many talks I have already delivered to you in my mind
can be summed up in two paragraphs.

One goes like this: To those of you who work in HIV and
AIDS-related programmes and are exposed to strange reac-

tions from your best friends, from your own relatives, from colleagues and bosses, from the system as a whole, please hold your hurt and anger for a moment. Let us look at it together and assume that all this is not necessarily ill will. All this has to do with powerful unconscious forces in us; it has to do with the group unconscious. As Freud taught us, the unconscious is neither good nor bad. The effects of its operations can be either. Sometimes in order to prevent it from causing havoc among us, we have to watch it.

My other speech is addressed to those group analysts who shy back from what they see as far too fashionable a field. I want to say this. A group-analytic view is badly needed to understand the madness surrounding the human immunodeficiency virus. Your knowledge and skills are needed now. And if you don't want to get involved, but you are interested in theory, is there not a tremendous amount to be learnt from this crisis? Even if the rarely mentioned possibility occurs that the virus burns itself out, is this not a unique opportunity *now* to study what primitive reactions our human minds are able to produce?

The reality of the group unconscious and the crucial importance of boundaries are particularly relevant to the AIDS crisis. If we want to bring out the full healing power of any group, we have to take care of the group in a special way: the group has to be made aware of its own destructive and self-destructive impulses. This can only happen within safe boundaries.

Let us cast a group-analytic glance at the AIDS crisis. AIDS has been officially called the 'biggest public health crisis of this century' (Sir Donald Acheson, Chief Medical Officer at the DHSS). We can observe that it is also surrounded by destructive group phenomena. They have been observed in teaching situations and workshops. They might appear among us today. If they do, it is better that we should talk about them openly rather than try to deny them.

These phenomena are not obvious at first sight. They appear among dedicated people who want to prevent and alleviate the suffering caused by the illness. The destructive impulses of the group unconscious are activated from within, paralysing our ability to function effectively. They uncannily mirror in the social field the destructive tactics of the retrovirus from within the defensive system of the body.

Here are a few standard examples. Those who work in the respective fields will be familiar with them. They occur with exasperating regularity.

A well-qualified new staff member joins a team of AIDS workers. The members of the team work extremely hard, are mutually supportive as well as caring and loving towards the patients. Most of these are either very ill or dying. The atmosphere is warm and paradoxically happy. The new staff member has to learn a lot. No one has time to introduce her to the various procedures. She is learning by trial and error. She feels that tasks others do not like doing are given to her, that mistakes made by others are blamed on her, that more often than not she is treated as if she were stupid. One of her dreaded scenes is when two or three colleagues pass by briskly and laugh at a quick in-joke. Her presence is only noticed when they need her for some menial job. She is increasingly choked with anger, tense and less and less able to speak up for herself. Soon she becomes ill, working days are lost, and, finally, she leaves the job.

We can take the opposite example, which is also frequent.

A new member joins another small and dedicated team. Every member is aware of the shared responsibility of introducing him to the tasks and procedures. They pay attention to his needs and devote a great deal of their time to explaining everything to him. The net result is overtime work. One of the team members falls ill. The stress is increased, and tension is developing. As soon as the absent member half recovers and staggers back to work, another member falls ill. And so on.

In both examples, the destructive phenomena are the result of the group unconscious acting blindly. It by-passes the conscious awareness of its members. Both groups have developed what appears to be a high degree of group cohesion. Actually, it is an anxious clinging together, rather than cohesion. The group members are unable to tolerate their ambivalent feelings towards each other. The good feelings are split off from the bad ones in the group unconscious. The loving feelings remain directed towards each other and towards the dying patients. In the first case, the negative side of powerful emotions was displaced on to someone who tried to join them. In the second case, the group was determined to do the right things. Firm and thoughtful leadership within the team had counteracted the primitive impulse of fighting off the intruder. However, the unacknowledged negative feelings towards the new member and each other made the team literally ill.

Apart from the personal distress, such disruptions in the work cause endless problems, hindering the effective management of AIDS programmes.

One obvious answer is to set up staff support groups. Remarkably persistent efforts are made in this direction, which regularly fail. It has been reported recently that a team made not less than seven unsuccessful attempts at setting up a staff support group. One standard story goes as follows:

A group conductor from outside the system volunteers to help. The offer is accepted with gratitude, but it also mobilizes the same unconscious group resistances against the newcomer as we have seen before. The outsider's good intentions might be blocked long before the group can even start. For instance, there is no suitable room available for the planned staff support group, no time can be found during working hours, or everyone questions the need to attend regularly and punctually. A starting date is agreed, then cancelled, then another date is fixed and cancelled again . . . and so on. When one hurdle is over-come, another one crops up. Someone suggests that a staff member should act as group leader. The support group starts. However, its boundaries are unclear. There is trouble with confidentiality. Members of the group do not feel safe. The group cannot function in a truly supportive way, more and more members start missing sessions, and finally the support group falls apart.

What we see here is declared and sincere consensus on one level and unconscious group resistance on another. One frequent reason why a staff support group might cease to exist is that its conductor has no power to protect it against external attacks. On the simplest level, such interference could be the change of the group room by the institution without previous notice having been given to the conductor or someone extraneous knocking at the door while the group is in session. The recurrence of such apparently insignificant events might seriously damage the group's feeling of security. The group might laugh off similar acts of intrusion as being amusing, but the group's unconscious perceives them correctly as hostility, envy or jealousy coming from the unconscious of other groups within the institution. Without full managerial backing, the conductor might not be able to protect the group from such assaults.

Managers and co-ordinators of AIDS-programmes are themselves overstressed in their battle with mysterious institutional blockages and unexpected events. They encounter a variety of stumbling blocks at every step. That an experienced key member of staff suddenly falls ill, suffers 'burn-out' or leaves the job is just one example. Here is another.

The head of a community programme wrote in a letter in May (1987) that the training of home helps for people with AIDS was less than half the battle. It was found that 75% dropped out after training due to the anxieties of their partners. This particular manager concluded that spouses and partners of staff had to be included in the training programme as well.

Norman Fowler (then Minister of State for Health and Social Services) courageously declared at the beginning of 1987 that 'information is the only cure we have'. But is information alone a cure for such problems? Destructive impulses coming from the group unconscious do not listen to objective information. Attitudes do not necessarily correlate with relevant knowledge. Also, our attitudes might prevent the information from reaching us in the first place. Here is an example.

A large college appointed one of its teachers to act as AIDS information officer. She took up the job with enthusiasm and added it to her existing tasks. Her plan to give talks on AIDS to students and staff was approved. However, no time could be found for the talks to take place. She noticed that her colleagues' attitudes towards her had subtly changed. She learned that behind her back she was called 'the AIDS-lady'.

Institutions have their own unconscious. They often react by isolating the group or the individual who deals with AIDS. It is as if those fighting against the threat of AIDS have to be isolated together with the virus.

There is no ready-made answer to the question of why the topic of AIDS triggers off more irrational reactions than any other contemporary killer disease. Neither the agony it causes to the patients, their families and friends nor its spread seem to account for our crazy reactions to it.

I say 'our' because I personally experienced such a reaction inside myself. That I have not acted upon my own irrational terror is due to the fact that I could recognize the sudden panic as coming from my unconscious, but only just. It produced a ridiculously surrealistic dialogue in my head. The dialogue was so vivid that subsequently I could write it down. It was as if I had been split into two: a very frightened animal and a reasonably well-informed rational being. It happened on the bus on my way home from the hospital. There I had seen someone suffering from AIDS and had shaken hands with him. The fear started abruptly 20 minutes later and persisted, despite the fact that I kept on telling myself all the things I knew about the impossibility of catching the virus just by shaking hands. The fear lasted for an hour and then disappeared without trace. (See also end of this section.)

Afterwards I heard similar personal accounts, although they are not easy to come by. Naturally we are all ashamed of having to admit to such primitive reactions. I am most grateful to a young university graduate who told me her story.

I was standing in a corner at a party, holding and feeding my baby. An old friend of mine appeared in the doorway, saw me and came up to greet me. He was smiling warmly, happy to see me. I had heard from mutual friends that he was antibody positive. Far from wishing to avoid him, I felt the urge to run towards him, to greet him with a kiss on the cheek. I knew perfectly well that it was safe. Yet another part of me was overcome by a sudden blind terror for the baby. The most striking aspect of this brief experience was the feeling that I was torn apart by two opposite forces: wanting to go forward towards him and wanting to escape at the same time. In the end I did not kiss him and knew I had hurt him. A few months later he died.

These and other personal accounts have in common the following aspects:

1. the simultaneous presence of the irrational and the rational;
2. the feeling of being split inside oneself or being torn apart by two opposite forces;

3. the sudden appearance and the equally abrupt disappearance of the experience.

Researchers in the United States have identified various emotional reactions to AIDS, such as fear of the unknown, of contagion, of disfigurement, of dying, of death, and of homosexuality. It seems to me that these different types of fears are in themselves half-rationalizations, a mixture of the irrational and the rational. When listed like this, they do not account for the underlying, blind terror that can overwhelm even a perfectly well-informed and rational mind.

I believe that it is more than a fanciful idea of mine if I assume that HIV infection and AIDS trigger off in all of us an archaic animal fear. At a deep, primitive level of our animal nature, fear and anger are very close together. Not to recognize the repressed anger, not to bring it back to the group, not to try to understand the actual impulse underneath the seemingly plausible statements and convincing talk can be dangerous.

Another part of us is filled with compassion and the determination to help, to alleviate the suffering. We have to start to heal the split within ourselves and allow the group as a whole to help us. The healing power of the small group might enable us to hold together the painfully opposite feelings— hate as well as love; our helplessness, sorrow and anger. It is my hope that this might happen today in the small groups.

* * *

Here is my personal experience mentioned in the above talk, my first encounter with an AIDS patient, in full:

On a conscious level I was well prepared for it. I knew how, according to the available evidence, the virus can and cannot be transmitted. I was not afraid of meeting him. I was introduced, and we shook hands. He turned out to be a nice, fun-loving, witty young man with a touch of poetry in his way of speaking. He was good-looking, but so pitifully thin. He told me about the disfiguring swelling around his ears that had now vanished completely. He had felt a monster then. Yet he is still afraid of the mirror, of what he might see in its depths. . . . He was called by the ward sister for yet another test. With some regret, we quickly said good-bye. His handshake was warm and trusting. He went reluctantly, staring back at me with a hunted look. Feelings of tenderness, impotent frustration mixed with a strong sense of guilt, and the certainty that he will soon die swept through me. He and his destiny occupied my mind as I was going home. In the bus there was no place to sit. With my left hand I was holding on to the strap hanging from the iron bar above my head. A strange bodily sensation made me look down to my right. What I saw took me by complete surprise. There was my right arm oddly streched out in a straight line, with palm and fingers open, but inches away from my clothes. At the same time panicky sentences started crossing my mind in rapid succession: 'Don't touch anything!' 'Concentrate, don't touch your face!' 'Oh my God, how can I ever again wash without using my right hand?' 'How will I eat?' 'I cannot touch any food for the rest of my life.' I closed my right hand into a fist, apparently to make sure I could not touch anything. Seeing that, my rational self bounced back, shook off the spell and went to grab the panicked animal: 'This is idiotic!' 'Stop it!' 'Stop it now!!' I heard the frightened animal in me whimpering something back. Then in a rather reconciliatory tone I told it off again: 'Don't be silly!' 'You know that you cannot catch it by shaking hands!' and, finally, in an attempt at compromise: 'All right, I will wash my hand.' The other voice carried on, fractionally calmer, but still very frightened: 'What do I do? There is no disinfectant at home.' My mind was too congested to remember that no disinfectant was needed, that even HIV-infected blood can be made innocuous with a mixture of simple household bleach and water. Actually I did have bleach at home, but all that knowledge was blocked out from my conscious mind. My whole body was tense, and the right arm nearly paralysed with fear. On arrival home I washed my hands with soap. I washed them twice, and that was it. The whole phenomenon disappeared without further trace. I must point out that I am not prone to any irrational fears or phobias. On the contrary, my family and friends have often rebuked me for taking too many risks with my health and safety. The above experience left me disconcerted, ashamed of myself, my self-image shattered by the close encounter with a blind ancestral animal in me.

PART TWO

Group responses
to the AIDS crisis:
experiences from a workshop

CHAPTER FIVE

From the first idea to the final format

The aims of the workshop

In the following pages a detailed account is given of the workshop 'Group Responses to the AIDS Crisis' that took place on 5 December 1987. I attempt to describe its prehistory, all the steps taken, including the hurdles and pitfalls encountered in the course of long preparations. Hopefully others will learn something from these experiences and be better equipped to set up similar workshops.

What hardly changed in essence or wording after the first draft of the programme was submitted for the GAS Committee's approval in March 1987 were the aims of the workshop. They were announced as follows:

1. to explore group responses that occur in institutions and the community in relation to the spread of HIV/AIDS;
2. to enable workers to become more aware of their own responses and deepen their understanding;
3. to improve the ability of workers to contain the fear and the irrational reactions generated by contact with and around HIV/AIDS.

Please note that for brevity's sake in this and the following chapters the initials of staff members and speakers are used. The full names are given in appendix II.

The first ideas

The workshop's prehistory started at the precise moment when, in my friends' shaded summer house in the south of France, I saw a special issue of a news magazine. It was a graphically illustrated, well-documented report on the latest horror befalling humanity. That was in August 1985. I read it spellbound. It had a mysterious, terrifying fascination. This was a disease of our times, SIDA—AIDS, the acquired immune deficiency syndrome—a threat from within. Two scientific centres, one in France, the other in the United States, were already engaged in a bitter fight over who had identified the virus first and who was the legitimate god-father entitled to give it a name that would go down in history. Shall it be called LAV or HTLV-III? Then a description for the lay reader. The virus lodges itself in and uses the genetic makeup of the very cells that constitute the protective system of the body. Nothing happens for a long time. The human immunodeficiency virus is a lentivirus—one of the family of the retroviruses—that can remain dormant for years. Once the immune system is mobilized, the retrovirus starts sprouting, multiplying and destroying.

While I was unsuccessfully trying to grasp the complex mechanics of it, parallel images of modern destruction from within sprang to my mind. The other day a television thriller featured a police inspector whose job it was to investigate crime, but who used his special position to commit murders in his spare time and, most importantly, got away with it. Another image is that of the friendly young man next to us in the plane suddenly drawing a grenade and ordering all passengers to put up their hands. They stay like that, waiting, while those with the objectionable passports are being taken into the cockpit to be murdered. In our times there are missiles, antimissiles, anti-antimissiles, and . . . presumably ad infinitum, if we don't perish on the way. Doomsday thoughts. There are also heroes in spy stories being unmasked twice over and more, so that, in the end, one gives up hope in any defence system. It amounts to a disintegration of basic trust.

The growing publicity given to AIDS in the media kept me thinking of what might be going on behind the facts, figures and warnings. My thoughts turned to the heavy demand put on those who care for people with AIDS, their families, close friends and the hospital staff. Reports also showed some strange phenomena surrounding the AIDS crisis (chapter 14). I was soon to encounter them myself.

The first person to whom I talked about my newly found interest shrank back and gave me his verdict: 'Every normal person tries to keep away from AIDS as much as he can. One has to put as much distance between AIDS and oneself as possible'. The implication that I was not a 'normal' person was more puzzling than hurtful. It was clear that what made this colleague recoil was the sheer mention of the word 'AIDS'. Unburdened by any real knowledge about HIV infection or related problems, his stance was firm and final. Others reacted in a similar fashion.

The way in

My interest was drawn to the total situation and to the helpers. Relationships will threaten to break down. A wife or a parent might learn for the first time of the spouse's or the son's sexual habits when he is diagnosed to be antibody positive. A pregnant mother finds out that she is infected and might start hating the unborn child. The first manifestation of the illness might be dementia. There will be a number of apparently healthy, but mentally disturbed young people going around in the community. As the hospitals will not have the capacity to cope, more and more community care will be needed. However, far from being ready for this, the community is turning against the victims. Already medically unfounded, irrational fear of AIDS is so intense that hospitals have to take even those sufferers who do not need hospital treatment, but who have nowhere else to go because of their hostile environment. Another psychological problem is that the mental state of those who have been diagnosed HIV positive can accelerate the process by which the quality of their lives diminishes. It can also facilitate the development of full-blown AIDS. HIV and AIDS arouse deep and intense feelings of loss associated with death and disfigurement, loneliness, fear, rage, guilt and aversion against 'the sinners', the 'deviant'. Contact with AIDS sufferers is particularly stressful because it can and does stir up personal problems in any of these areas (Grey, 1987).

How will the helpers cope with the cumulative stress? The time had arrived when group-analytic knowledge and experience was needed on a large scale. How could we put the conceptual, therapeutic and experiential tools of group analysis at the helpers' disposal? Naturally, I thought, we at the Group-Analytic Society (GAS) and the Institute of Group Analysis (IGA) should organize special courses for those who do counselling before and after the HIV test, for those working in the primary care of AIDS patients, for administrators, managers, and trainers involved in HIV/AIDS-related programmes. Moreover, we should establish a network of group analysts prepared to conduct staff support groups, do supervision and act as resource persons. With these ideas in mind I approached the Society (GAS) and the Institute (IGA) early in 1987, made many telephone calls and wrote to all the key people. A variant of that letter went to the editors of *Dialogue*, the IGA newsletter. An appeal to colleagues under the heading 'Information Exchange to Help the Helpers of AIDS Sufferers' was published alongside the letter. We also pinned it on the blackboard of the Institute. It remained there for months. The net result was one single telephone call by a colleague, CR, whom I had not met before, and we exchanged our experiences in this field.

The official response was more positive, albeit somewhat cautious. In its meeting of 11 March, the GAS Committee gave the go-ahead to organize a one-day workshop to bring together interested group analysts with people on the front-line of the AIDS crisis. The Scientific Programme Committee of IGA in its meeting of 15 July agreed that the workshop should be a joint GAS/IGA event. The issue of training needs related to the AIDS crisis had been put on the agenda of the IGA Training Committee.

At the same time I started to make the first contacts with individuals and agencies involved with HIV/AIDS-related programmes. Because most of the people in this field were extremely busy, being unable to refrain from overcommit-ting their time and working beyond endurance, many of my letters were answered with great delay and some not at all. Any first reaction I received to my offer of group-analytic help was genuinely positive. Then usually nothing hap-pened, or the contact was slowly but surely lost. In several cases the initial invitation to send a representative to our workshop was countered months later by another invitation to me to attend a workshop or conference on HIV/AIDS set up by the same organization, the cooperation of which I had sought in the first place. . . .

In May, DE and I succeeded in making the crucial link with one of the hospitals leading this field, and I started attending one of their weekly meetings in June. To make sure that I did not miss anything essential, in June I also enrolled in a five-day course on AIDS counselling given by one of the counselling organizations, and I began conducting support groups for staff working as HIV test counsellors and with AIDS patients in two hospitals in July and October. In the course of this work I gained invaluable further insights into the intricacies of group responses to the stress caused by HIV and AIDS.

During all this time I searched the news and the literature. On the occasion of a few short visits (on other business) to

Denmark, Germany and Spain I gathered information on how the AIDS crisis is dealt with in those countries and above all how individuals, groups and the public at large react to it. On the whole, I was struck more by the similarities than by the differences in the reactions.

Towards the final format

The team was formed in a very short space of time. All those asked responded with enthusiasm. Two changed their minds and could be replaced early on. We were lucky enough to have MP as chairman, JB and DE (Tavistock Clinic) as co-convenors. Without their help and support we could not have achieved what we did. As for the group conductors, preference was given to those who already had some experience in this field. In the end, the seven small groups were conducted by AMh, CR, DE, DV, JBa, JG and JH. The team was kept up to date with developments mostly by telephone and correspondence. Relevant articles, a glossary and a bibliography were circulated.

After having prepared a tentative draft of the workshop's programme, we had a first crucial meeting between the convenors, the chairman and one of the would-be speakers at the end of March. That meeting left me so frustrated and exhausted that I nearly gave up. Two other people whom we had invited could not join us. One of those who were present arrived very late, having misunderstood my instructions about the venue. Or had I unwittingly given unclear instructions? The meeting tended to be blocked by one person, and when I put forward a date in June for the workshop to be held, I was unanimously voted down. There was anxiety and a general feeling, which I did not share, that we were not yet ready to do it so soon. Afterwards, I had to remind myself of the positive outcome of the meeting—that a definite date had been fixed and the programme approved.

That I did not share my colleagues' anxiety was only true in the sense that at the time I completely ignored my own internal reactions. What I felt deep down was irrelevant to me then. I only wanted us to forge ahead and organize the workshop as soon as possible. I was tense with an enormous impatience. The cumulative effect of that continuing tension might partly account for the severe physical disability I suffered two weeks before the workshop. It compelled me to hand over the remaining tasks completely to JB, DE and MP. In the event, after a few days of immobility, I was able to resume the work. Of course, by then my impairment had caused additional anxiety to my colleagues.

There were a couple more meetings between us, the convenors, and innumerable consultations on the phone. The whole team held a final meeting a week before the workshop. We discussed every minute aspect of the programme and the difficulties to be anticipated in the small groups as well as in the plenary sessions. Moreover, we made last-minute modifications and assigned our respective roles (appendix III). In this briefing session the importance of time-keeping during the workshop was emphasized in relation to every point discussed. JB took upon herself the unglamorous chore of making the announcements and monitoring that every detail went according to plan. Her invisible role was hopefully going to give the rest of us enough freedom from anxiety to concentrate exclusively on our respective tasks.

After this preparatory meeting, the final version of the programme was distributed to the group conductors. The first draft of the programme had been followed by seven subsequent ones, each submitted for comments to the co-convenors and the chairman. The title of the workshop was changed a couple of times, mostly in order to avoid using words that might hurt various sensitivities. What caused most difficulties and disagreements was the question of whether to have feedback from the small groups to the plenary session and if so, in which form. Decisions were made and reversed several times (chapter 8). The finer points of the organization (e.g., time needed to make announcements or to move from one part of the premises to another) were also thought through. Nothing was left to chance. Not surprisingly, we ended up with two programmes—a short one for the participants (appendix V) and another for the organizers, with all the details we had worked out (appendix IV).

CHAPTER SIX

Participants, staff and the spirit of the workshop

As a result of many personal contacts, hundreds of telephone calls and the mailing of a vast number of selectively targeted registration forms (appendix Ib), a steady stream of applications began to come in from mid-September onwards. To our delight, they all seemed to be people who wanted to join for the same reasons that lay behind our setting up the workshop. Its aims did appeal to the kind of persons we wanted to attract. Two eminent experts in the field who could not come because of their engagements abroad sent most encouraging letters of support.

Altogether, we were 60 people in the workshop, including the speakers, the chairman, the group conductors and the convenors. Participants came not only from London, but from all over the country (Brighton, Cambridge, Lancaster, Leeds, Leicester) and even from Denmark and Spain. Most participants had either a vast (60%) or some (25%) knowledge and experience of HIV and/or AIDS-related programmes. Only a minority (15%) were new to this field. There were 12 doctors, 27 nurses, health advisers and other primary care workers. The composition of the workshop was nearly exactly as planned. Nevertheless, the fact that only 7 group analysts applied to join us and 4 of them subsequently withdrew is rather puzzling. In the end there were 13 group analysts altogether (including 10 staff members!).

Last-minute cancellations were more numerous than are usual in IGA/GAS workshops. A high rate of drop-outs has been noticed in other meetings, too, in which the topic is AIDS or other equally anxiety-provoking subjects having to do with dying and death. The maximum number of planned participants (69) was reached by the end of October. We were able to replace early cancellations by telephoning those who had not been accepted because we were fully booked. But some of those whom we called had already made other arrangements. Moreover, a number of participants simply did not turn up on the day.

There were others whom I had attempted to include, but without success—for instance, lawyers and life insurance people who deal with cases involving HIV/AIDS. Admittedly, they had not been listed in our leaflet (appendix Ia) among the categories of people to whom the workshop was recommended. A representative of The Haemophiliac Society registered, but he cancelled his participation only a few days before the workshop. A participant lamented the absence of self-help group speakers and black AIDS workers.

Whoever was there seemed to contribute to a very warm and friendly ambiance. The chairman and the three convenors had waived any fees for their work and time invested. Not to do so seemed to contradict the spirit of the workshop. This spirit was characterized by self-restraint, dedication to the task and mutual support, which was evident already in the above-described staff briefing meeting before the workshop. It permeated the whole event. The friendliness of the catering staff was explicitly praised by several participants. The bookstall was a useful and interesting feature, also adding to the congenial atmosphere.

The people who made the workshop were, of course, the participants. Many of them valued the breaks, during which they could have contact with each other and brief insights into each others' work. Here are a few comments written by participants after the workshop and giving glimpses into the spirit of the place:

'Impressive to see the wide range of skills, concern, commitment, dedication and dogged hard work that is there in the lives of the carers, a richness in their personalities and points of view. I greatly appreciated and enjoyed the contributions people made, unaware for the most part of how much of themselves they were giving. Uplifting.'

'[It was interesting] that participants came from so many different areas of work.'

'I experienced a very warm and supportive atmosphere at the workshop.'

'It was good to meet up with some other gay therapists who are trying to use analytic concepts in the gay community as it attempts to respond to the AIDS/HIV crisis.'

'It was good to talk personally with people I'd only contacted on the phone before! The feeling that there are people who care about AIDS and want to help, helped me feel less isolated.'

'During the coffee and lunch breaks I chatted with other participants. I was struck by the awe-inspiring dedication of people who are working in day-to-day contact with AIDS sufferers. They seemed to me to have a tremendous sense of purpose and meaning in their lives. One of them said, "I can't remember what life was like before AIDS". I wondered about the flip-side of this experience. There was no time in the coffee break to explore this further, but during the rest of the day I certainly gained some insight into it.'

CHAPTER SEVEN

The four talks

T he day started with four talks. It was our intention to select the topics and the speakers in such a way that a wide spectrum of points of view would be conveyed to the participants. All speakers were asked to present their own personal experiences as far as they felt it was possible to do so in an open forum. We deliberately avoided giving factual information about HIV infection, its history, current spread, prospects of prevention and cure. The aim was to concentrate on the psychological and social aspects and, more specifically, on the emotional experiences surrounding the AIDS crisis as well as the concomitant group phenomena that might be hampering the implementation of the necessary preventative and treatment measures. From all accounts the talks did achieve their intended purpose. The following is a summary by Sarah T. Willis, one of the participants.

Introductory talk

by Malcolm Pines

Malcolm Pines explored the way we use language around illness and disease and our concepts of healing. He showed how we are all 'suspended in a linguistic, symbolic universe' and that we give symbolic meanings to our experience of illness that bring together the cognitive and the affective, the physical states and the social responses. For instance, illness used to be defined as synonymous with evil. We can imagine how such a symbolic meaning must affect the various levels of response to the 'patient'. The semantic web that underlies our attitudes is close to the matrix of the illness. AIDS occurs when there is a breakdown of immunological competence in the person. How are we responding to this illness—MP asked—and is there some link between the answer to this and the fact that the illness appears to mirror a breakdown in the psycho-social, cultural experience of society?

'The power of groups'

by Angela Molnos

The tone for reflection and exploration in the workshop was set by Angela Molnos. She drew attention to the splits that occur in institutions, groups and individuals when primitive reactions of fear and rage are triggered by AIDS. AM led the search by suggesting that first we need to heal the split within ourselves. The full text of her talk can be found in chapter 4.

'Reactions in and around a hospital's AIDS team'

by Charles Farthing

Charles Farthing spoke with alarming familiarity about his daily life lived in close proximity with the AIDS virus. He began by describing a typical person with AIDS as someone who may have concurrently five complex diseases, has lost his job, and his parents have just found out he is gay. If CF spends half an hour with such a person, he is accused by his colleagues of 'spoiling' his patients. 'You think they're so special? . . . You think *you're* so special!' He encounters a wide range of responses to himself and the work he does. He gave us a fascinating glimpse into the myriad emotional tones of such group responses. He meets with resentment, adulation and envy from colleagues in other teams within the same hospital. They often want to see AIDS as 'just another disease' and demonstrate a huge resistance against specialized AIDS teams. [It was very interesting to hear, I thought, how concrete are the efforts to deny fear. CF believes that the publicity machine has been very influential in all this. It struck me as ironic that the attempts of the media to alert us to the dangers of this epidemic might actually have increased our resistance to improving our capacity to find an appropriate response to such an illness.]

He went on to talk about life in the wards and graphically described how mood shifts occur in a terrible downward spiral. For some time there may be levity, humour, love and spontaneity. The ward is a happy place. People get to know each other. The patients and staff groups are cohesive and supportive. Then, as the staff get busier and busier, deaths accumulate, morale slips, workers become exhausted and feel they have no more to give. They suffer from a lack of validation and appreciation from those above. They are told they haven't done enough, that they are failing, that they're not doing the right things—and people go on dying. Staff are overstretched and overstressed, and each individual seeks his disburdenment alone.

Some doctors choose to work in this field in order to make money, opportunistically seeking an advantage where there is weakness and vulnerability. This reminded me of what AM had said about how destructive forces in the wider society seem to reflect the destructive tactics of the virus. CF views this behaviour as a gross example of mass hypocrisy. [I think that his view is valid, but I wonder if the appeal of this notion—to me, at least—suggests with what ease we split ourselves into good and bad—even good and bad doctors.]

There is so much fear around. The patients even fear that their doctors, whom they are learning to trust, will take control away from them. For this reason alone they may prevaricate and resist accepting AZT treatment. CF told us how he has witnessed the universal fear of infectivity. Interestingly, he went on immediately to describe the hatred and mistrust of homosexuality. He said 'It is as if society teaches people to dislike homosexuals.' Much of the counselling work is around this issue, especially with parents. They have to be discouraged from expressing their loathing of homosexuality to their dying sons. The patients dread this confrontation with their parents often more than they dread death itself. On the AIDS ward real fear and paranoid projections coalesce. CF's juxtaposition of fear of infectivity and hatred and mistrust of homosexuality highlights how people do not just loathe homosexuals because they fear catching AIDS from them; they loathe and vilify homosexuals anyway. It draws attention to the scapegoating mechanism that was already in operation even before the advent of AIDS into the homosexual community. This juxtaposition also made me think that society has always taught people to fear catching homosexuality, as if it were an infectious disease. I began to see that the fear of infectivity appears to be linked in our collective unconscious with the fear of increasing, uncontrolled moral degeneracy.

'People like us need protection from people like you.' CF finished his talk with a quote from an unsigned letter he had received. Such a remark indicates the unconscious process by which those fighting this illness become equated with the illness itself.

Finally, CF turned to an examination of the responses of the opinion-forming bodies, notably the press and the churches. He demonstrated how split the reactions are— accepting and supportive on the one hand (there are huge numbers of volunteers offering help), judgemental and condemning on the other. He observed: 'Information becomes misinformation under the influence of social dynamics.'

[CF's eloquent and passionately felt talk stirred up some anxiety in me, the writer of this account, and presumably in others present. He told several joky anecdotes which, although true, seemed to exaggerate the awful, destructive bigotry that is around. We laughed in recognition and relief, maybe because we needed to grant ourselves the momentary deception that the capacity for all this destructiveness could not possibly be in us too.]

'The AIDS crisis and society at large'

by Antony Grey

Antony Grey developed the notion of AIDS as a seminal, social problem. He introduced his talk with the idea that AIDS has the potential for either bringing about a greater degree of social cohesion or splitting us up into warring factions.

He explored the roots of paranoia, the splitting, denial and projection that go on all around us as we avoid grappling with the psychological impact of the AIDS threat. There is a 'toxic time bomb' among us. We are living in an age of uncertainty, tension and anger because of the loss of confidence in our own and each other's healthiness. People need to be close, mentally and emotionally. How can we be this now? One solution is to split people into two groups: the healthy and responsible, the unhealthy and irresponsible. Phobic and paranoid thinking dominate the scene. Marginalized groups, homosexuals and drug misusers, conveniently and tragically present themselves as scapegoats for these projections.

In looking more closely at how these mechanisms operate, AG reminded us that often people set out as rescuers, become persecutors and in due course become victims themselves. In the 'dramatic triangle' people dance an endless waltz (Karpman, 1968). AG drew our attention to the book *Folk Devils and Moral Panics* by Stanley Cohen (1973), from which we might learn more about how the agents of moral indignation generate anxiety, concern and panic.

Great antipathy has been stirred up against gays. [As I listened to his speech, I began to realize that in society at large—just as in the hospital—the big bogey to many people is the deviancy that the illness seems to be attached to and not AIDS itself. AG confirmed what I have observed in my work, that those heterosexuals who hate their own sexuality often project this hatred onto gay people. In the AIDS epidemic lawyers, police and insurance brokers institutionalize such attitudes.]

He drew a parallel and made links between difficulties surrounding racist attitudes and those surrounding feelings generated towards AIDS sufferers. Communication becomes fraught with danger. You hesitate to voice your opinion that the illness came from primates in Africa, because you might be told you are being racist. No one sees logic. Everybody feels blamed.

AG told us of a newspaper report about a priest who declared he was prepared to shoot his son if he had AIDS. And his son said, 'Sometimes I think my father would like to shoot me, whether I had AIDS or not'. AG, like CF, used humour to illustrate some of his points, and to reach out to us over the anxiety and dread.

He had looked closely at the group pathology of AIDS. He described the operational 'warring factions' of his thesis, but he did not explore at all his alternative notion of the poten-

tial for the achievement of 'a greater degree of social cohesion'. [I found myself feeling a bit let down by this.] He
finished his talk by reminding us that 'sick' was once used to
mean 'criminal' and 'stealing' and that this equation unfor-
tunately still holds today. [I became aware of how urgently
we need to address the tangled web of unconscious assumptions that underlie the AIDS crisis.]

CHAPTER EIGHT

The unspeakable emerges from the non-fishbowl

At this stage the reader might want to look up the workshop programme in appendices IV and V to see the sequence of events. After the four talks participants were divided into small groups (chapter 9). Half-way through their experiential group work—that went on up to the concluding plenary session— there was a special kind of feedback session. It is this feedback that is described in the present chapter.

The bridge between the small groups and the workshop as a whole

The question whether we wanted feedback from the small groups or not, and if so, in what form, was the object of many discussions among the organizers before the workshop. Several suggestions were made, modified and rejected. The usual format, which requires appointed representatives of the small groups to stand up in the plenary session and use 4 to 5 minutes each to report one after the other on their respective groups, was the first to be discarded. Such reports are invariably dull, repetitive and often only meaningful for those who had been in the particular group. They tend to concentrate on the topics discussed, without reflecting the group's particular atmosphere, its dynamics and the uniqueness of a session. Another idea was that the group conductors would form a small group in the centre, surrounded by concentric circles of seats occupied by all others who would listen in silence for 40 minutes. The conductors would talk about their own personal experience of their small groups, their own feelings and anxieties. This suggestion was immediately blocked by one of the conductors, who felt that such a personal exposure would make her very vulnerable. Others argued against it on nearly the opposite grounds, i.e., that it would give too much power and importance to the conductors. I was not convinced by either of these arguments, but I had to give way.

The finally agreed format was as follows. Towards the end of the morning session the conductors would ask the groups to appoint a representative to report to the plenary session after lunch. Perhaps mistakenly it was left to the group conductor to decide how to explain to the group the mechanics of the reporting. Most conductors did not say that this reporting would be done by the representatives sitting in a circle surrounded by the rest of the participants, who were asked to keep silent. Also somehow the term fishbowl was mentioned, alongside goldfishbowl, although we knew full well that this was a misnomer. It is true that the term fishbowl is applied to a variety of formats, but none of them appears to be group-analytic. In fact, in the Stockholm conference of 1978 (E. Foulkes; Lear, 1979) it was decided that the fishbowl was contrary to group analysis. The term fishbowl has been applied to a central small group sitting in a circle with a vacant chair and without a conductor. The group is surrounded by a large silent audience. If someone from the audience wants to contribute to the small group's discussion, he will have to get up from his seat, go to the centre, take the empty chair and speak. After having made his contribution, he has to return to his original seat, and someone else from the audience will take advantage of the vacant place in the centre. Sometimes there is a second chair kept empty for someone else from the audience waiting his turn as the first one still speaks. Another format consists of a central group that has the task of enacting or dramatizing a theme on behalf of the large group as a whole. The format we adopted was quite different. It had a conductor and was conducted along group-analytic lines. I prefer to call it the 'non-fishbowl'.

The conductor's personal account

At 1:40 p.m. we started warning participants that the plenary session was about to begin. The first session of the seven small groups had taken place after the talks between 11:15 and 12:45. JB and I spent that time in the library, which was our staff room. Now the delicious cold salad lunch was over, and the empty plates had already disappeared, thanks to BL's magic organization. People were mingling and chatting. Some were caught up in the room near the main entrance, where an employee of our local bookshop specializing in psychotherapy had displayed the classic volumes of group analysis and the few publications available on the psychological aspects of HIV/AIDS. A couple of colleagues passed by, signalling to me with a glance of encouragement and a gesture hinting at success that the workshop was going very well. I smiled back in gratitude, but now I had to concentrate on what was to come.

Soon the large room was full. In its middle, a circle of eight empty chairs was surrounded by further circles of participants taking up their seats. I moved resolutely towards the inner circle. Two or three women followed me, and we sat down. The other chairs, including the ones next to me right and left, remained vacant for an agonizingly long couple of minutes. It crossed my overstretched mind that one or more group representatives might simply fail to turn up, having gone for an after-lunch walk instead. However, the seats began to be occupied. A man opposite me started saying that this was not what he had expected. He was anxious, and his words faded away. MP, the chairman, gave the general instructions as agreed—namely, that we had 40 minutes during which the representatives in the fishbowl would talk. All others around were asked to keep silent. He would warn us 5 minutes before the time was over. I felt uncomfortable hearing him use the term fishbowl. While he was talking, the last two members arrived hurriedly, and the circle was complete.

In my capacity as the conductor of this special small group, I introduced the session. I tried to be brief and strictly truthful by spelling out that we, the organizers, had opted for this format in order to enable all participants to share by proxy something of their small group experiences. I added that the present format, which we had chosen in preference to others, had its problems too. The members of the central circle might feel anxious, watched and criticized by those around us. Some might feel that they could not disclose certain information about their own group. I suggested therefore that everyone should feel completely free to report whatever appears appropriate to him or her in this situation, or to withhold information, or to talk on his or her own behalf only. Someone who was in the audience wrote after the workshop that I was apologizing for setting up the fishbowl. That, of course, was not my intention, but I might have sounded hesitant.

As soon as I finished, the member on my left started talking. He said that he did not dream of disclosing anything about his group and only intended to talk on his own behalf. Then the vivacious young lady next to him gave us a brisk report and what seemed to be the version authorized by her group. All those in the circle talked one after the other, in clockwise order. They took up a couple of minutes each. Despite the different styles of reporting and the varying contents, the whole thing sounded monotonous. Actually, it was very much like the usual small group reports in a plen-

ary session that the organizers had wanted to avoid. It was
hard to concentrate on what was being said. Only a statement by the anxious man stood out: he felt he was betraying
his small group by talking about them here, so publicly.

When they had all finished, there was a moment of very
tense silence. I remarked that the lack of structure in this
group created anxiety, that they unwittingly were clinging
to a familiar format—reporting in a most orderly fashion one
after the other—as a defence against the shared anxiety and
that the problem now was what to do next. The lady to my
right expressed her great anxiety. I joined her by saying that
I felt the same. Actually my heart was pounding uncontrolla-
bly at that point. I felt it was responding directly to a mounting massive panic in the group's unconscious. Others talked
about their anxiety. Someone tried to stick to the 'task' by
asking questions about others' groups. After a few half-
hearted exchanges the attempt petered out. I noted that we
could not go forward unless we dealt with the feelings in the
here-and-now first. There were remarks about those outside
our circle who sat in silence, listening, and the question was
asked what they might think of us. This was countered by the
young doctor on my left. He felt reassured, supported by the
presence of the members of his small group somewhere in the
background.

Then a middle-aged man spoke, firmly and clearly. His
brief speech unleashed and condensed the drama of the
whole workshop and beyond. He said he needed to be the
centre of attention, he wanted to be creative. He wanted to do
so much, he was still young and yet there was so little time
left. He was dying of AIDS. In the limited time he still had he
wanted to make his mark. He craved for power to do things.
Then, suddenly, realizing that he did have power, he lifted
his hand as if holding a deadly weapon above our heads. He
talked about this syringe full of blood with which he could
make his mark, teach a lesson to all those who claim that
they are the helpers, the carers.

I ceased to listen at this point because of a great anger
mounting in me. My anger was not about his symbolic

threat. Or perhaps it was. It might have been my primitive reaction to a primordial threat to my existence, to the existence of the human race. For a few dreadful seconds, the ground under me was shifting as if in an earthquake. I was angry and totally unable to decide whether this was just play-acting or whether he really was HIV positive or had AIDS. My thoughts collided inside my head. If he is actually carrying the virus, everything in this room would change, within and without the circle. If not, why does he . . . , how does he dare to play with the idea? Others around me probably have similar thoughts to mine in this very moment. I must do something. Recovering my strength, I decided to meet him head on: 'Wait a minute. Are you saying that . . . that you are really . . . ?' He responded with a slight shaking of his head. A second wave of anger swept through my body. In what I hoped was an objective and yet supportive voice, I told him that I experienced anger with him for pretending to be a PWA. I felt and spoke as if that status were sacred, too serious to be played with. His imagery indicated enormous rage and hatred, and I was wondering whether he was angry with the organizers of this workshop, i.e. with me here-and-now. He coyly denied it. However, he added that he found it difficult to acknowledge his feelings face-to-face with the other person. He mentioned that he had come late to this group because he had been lingering around the stalls, burying himself in books as usual, rather than dealing with real emotions.

While all this was going on, there was silence and tense attention around us. I was aware of a couple of group conductors behind me keenly watching our interactions and felt supported by their concentration. Somewhere towards the periphery of the large group a man and a woman were passing joky comments to each other and giggling, but I was not aware of that. I was told about it only afterwards by various participants who had been greatly irritated by those two. In front of me, a few concentric rows beyond the centre, I saw our chairman apparently gently nodding off. I remembered having seen him do just that in other meetings and then all of a sudden jump back to his former imposing presence and speak very much to the point, as if he had heard everything. The lady to my right remarked that it was reassuring to see someone fall asleep. It meant that things were alright, safe, there was nothing to be anxious about.

Towards the end the vivacious young lady said that she did not like to link HIV/AIDS too much with death. We all are condemned to die. She wanted to talk about living with AIDS. At this stage the non-fishbowl was a truly experiential group. My voice had become muted, barely audible beyond the central circle. Perhaps I started protecting us from those outside our small group. Returning from his apparent slumber, our chairman announced with unfailing precision: 'Five minutes more', and soon after that it was over.

This session made a profound impression on me. It was so burningly alive at the time that I did not bother to write it down. I reacted as if I could not possibly ever forget it—an indelible memory engraved upon my mind, a succession of thoughts, a swell of anxiety and emotions that could always be recalled.

The non-fishbowl seen by a participant
Account by Sarah T. Willis

The same event has been described by STW, one of the participants, who has been taking notes while the non-fishbowl was going on. The reader might find it interesting to compare our accounts written independently from each other.

Although AM introduced the fishbowl by saying that it was not meant to be an experiential group, it evolved into something that looked like one. Here were seven people struggling with feelings associated with being put on the spot. They expressed, in turn, annoyance, embarrassment, fear and paranoia. It had the appearance of an intimate group, and yet it felt neither intimate nor private. Here they were, surrounded by a fascinated public (maybe 50 people), observed in all their vulnerability, without a script, and apparently with no sense of what they were 'supposed' to do. They had done as they were told, and now they were experiencing resistance and dismay. Was all this a set-up? Did the Institute (of Group Analysis) plan the two empty chairs? Who had died? There was an alarm bell ringing outside. Several fantasies developed, the strongest of which seemed to be the idea that here we had a group of people all dying of AIDS. One representative felt he was letting his small group down. Another felt torn away from the comfort of his small group. So what were we onlookers? The horrified family, or the persecuting masses? I felt upset by my inability to reach out and talk to them. After all, only those in the middle were supposed to speak: I, too, was obeying the rules.

The representatives talked about acquiring a new identity; it was as if they had been antibody positive and now they knew they had AIDS. Someone said: 'I don't know what I'm here for. Am I here for me, or for my group?' And there followed a general grumbling about the fact that they had been given no clear brief. This intensified and became real anger, which appeared in the form of a fantasy of power and destruction. This was expressed so vividly that it was fleetingly difficult to sort out fact from fantasy. I had the impression that we were engaging in a kind of crazy role-play or psychodrama that teetered on the edge of reality. Did someone in the fishbowl really have AIDS? The representatives toyed with the idea of what they would do with so little time left to live: wreak enormous damage, make a mark, squeeze out for themselves all the loving they had never had, 'make the bastards pay', be remembered? 'We could be deviant. We don't have to sit here obediently waiting to die. We could attack them with an infected needle.' In the 'audience' I felt confronted by a dying person's helplessness. AM, who was by now talking very quietly, suggested that we all need to be in touch with our own helplessness. Deep inside me I heard the distant echo of my own.

I thought I picked up the underlying fantasy of an omnipotent and homicidal parent, threatening to kill and maybe devour the helpless and vulnerable infant. What led me to see this was a series of events in my small group now echoed in the fishbowl. Mothers talked of their fears for their grown-up children and even their unborn children. 'I'm so worried about my son who is sexually active and in New York.' Then, 'If I had a child, I'd dread giving AIDS to it.' The group felt eaten up by the doctor-, parent-figures. Could these concerns disguise the even greater dread of a parent's capacity to kill, maim, attack or withhold love? The joke about the son who said about his father, 'maybe he wanted to kill me whether I had AIDS or not' aroused the heartiest laugh of the day. Some of the day's imagery was about dropping bombs. I wondered, what about dropping babies?

The rage expressed in the fishbowl was directed at the convenor, i.e., AM. People felt they had been set up. AM, in her capacity as the conductor of the fishbowl, interpreted appositely: 'I think you are angry with the organizer, that is, with me.' People were angry at mother for putting them here in this (life-) threatening predicament. Earlier she had spoken of the conductor's powerlessness in the hospital to protect the staff support group from external attacks. What seemed to be happening now in this group's unconscious fantasy was the powerlessness of the conductor to protect the group from the mother's own destructive urges. 'You put us here and now you are making us suffer', was the feeling. The threat was in the primary union with mother.

Such a powerful fantasy doesn't seem to me so far-fetched in the context of the AIDS issue. Sexual intercourse, which once brought anticipation of bliss and the possibility of life and new hope, now brings this together with terror, suspicion and sometimes death. An awesome combination—small wonder if we resort to some primitive fantasy of infanticide which links birth and death in a compelling way.

This experience of the fishbowl may well have been the least clearly defined part of the day, but it turned out to encapsulate for me the loss of order and control that is central to the experience of AIDS, and also some of the polarities that characterize our response to this catastrophic illness. Here was a group of people participating in the Workshop, cooperating with the timetable of the day, politely following the unspoken rules. Then, suddenly for a moment something happened in the fishbowl, and there wasn't any clarity, nobody knew the rules, everything became uncertain and frightening. A situation of dis-ease had come upon us. Those who were onlookers continued to obey the demands of convention, but in doing so felt powerless and pushed away. Those who were in the centre creatively adapted to the exigences of their new situation, gaining strength in the face of doubt and uncertainty. The link between the two groups of people was the feelings that we all shared, mediated by the conductor: our anger, helplessness, fear and alienation; and our longing for intimacy and life itself. I felt that in this fishbowl we came some way towards healing the split in ourselves, which AM had talked about at the beginning of the day (chapter 4).

Other participants' responses

The contrasting variety of reactions, not only within the inner circle, but also among those who were silently watching us, is revealed by many spontaneous remarks about this non-fishbowl session written in response to the evaluation questionnaire. Here are the participants' written responses:

'The fishbowl provoked a wide range of feelings in me, in particular the man who described himself with the syringe full of blood. My feelings were those of anxiety and anger, I guess. I haven't yet figured this out!'

'It was quite interesting to see the various reactions of the "representatives" to finding themselves in this unexpected situation. The member from our own group said later that she found the fishbowl actually less anxiety-provoking than if she had been required to stand up in front of everybody and report. As for myself, I was in the audience, wondering why do I often find it hard not to say something when silence is expected? My spontaneity and rebelliousness seem to be stimulated in this situation.'

'"Goldfish bowl" very interesting but high-handed. Fascinating but remote. In such a hothouse what is valid?'

'It was fascinating to see the small groups becoming the fishbowl in the midst of the large group. What happened there was very brain-boggling. I don't think I could describe how or why. Also, I'm not sure that I would want to recall or identify in detail what actually went on. I'd rather leave it as it was. A lot was happening, and it was a powerful experience.'

'I liked the fishbowl group very much and thought it was useful. It also aroused some anxiety, especially the man who phantasized being HIV positive and giving it to people with the infected needle. I would repeat the fishbowl in a future workshop.'

'There were very powerful feelings in response to the fishbowl and small group experiences that surprised me. I think it must have to do with AIDS which stimulates "primitive" feelings.'

'It was uncomfortable to discover my own reaction at the beginning of the fishbowl: quite smug and patronizing, I was glad it wasn't me. A good lesson.'

'The goldfishbowl was very powerful.'

'I was struck by the identification of one member of the fishbowl group with the fear, rage and hatred raised in victims against the helpers and society. If it is considered necessary to represent the findings of small groups in the plenary, then some other format has to be found.'

'I had not heard of the fishbowl before and hence had no idea what to expect when I agreed to provide our small group's feedback. I found it quite exciting despite the performance anxiety it engendered in me—possibly because AM was conducting it and I had valued her opening remarks, possibly because my natural talkativeness was being indulged!'

'The post-lunch fishbowl which I had felt some apprehension about was very skilfully led by AM. In a symbolic way the "drama" performed in the group seemed to contain the kind of acting out associated with AIDS workshops—identification with the victim. It had a positive effect on the subsequent small group and the constructive debate in the final plenary meeting.'

'The goldfishbowl I found disturbing as we had been led to believe the feedback would be different. It took me some time to calm down and to take in what was happening. I felt so sorry for my representative and glad it wasn't me!'

'The fishbowl was valuable and thought-provoking. AM was a very good facilitator—The member who represented our group in the fishbowl felt really in the hot seat. He had no idea it would feel like that.'

'Poor procedural organization behind the fishbowl group created unnecessary bad feeling.'

'I felt very angry about the fishbowl at the time and still feel the organizers lost a lot of trust at this point in the day— because of a feeling of deception—which I think was quite unnecessary. If we had been told that we may be asked to do something unexpected at any point in the day it would have been fine.'

'The fishbowl group session was useful and positive, but not necessarily pleasant!'

'I found the fishbowl fascinating as an analyst, but very worrying as a workshop participant.'

'I did not feel the fishbowl session was very useful. I think a more formal report from each group leader might have been better with a general discussion from the floor.'

'I found the goldfishbowl experience disappointing and tho' I could see there were valid reasons for choosing this format, I would probably have preferred a theme-centred plenary discussion.'

'It may be that the speakers and the participants in the goldfish bowl were setting a culture for the day which could contain the phobic panic. They appeared empowered by their position or by the sense of the backing of their small group to transform the mindless panic society experiences into thoughtful discussion of paranoid fears which have become associated with death, homosexuality and contagion.'

Group-analytic considerations

Reviewing these reports and personal reactions to our non-fishbowl, the one common view that emerges is that it was powerful. A few group analysts attempted to explain this experience that seemed to elude most participants' rational analysis. Three comments especially stand out:

First of all there is the observation by STW that there were underlying unconscious fantasies of infanticide. This shocking idea seems to hold the key to the apparently mysterious power of the experience. The format must have mobilized horrific unconscious fantasies about infanticide perpetrated by mother because of a double emotional parallel. For one, of course, the virus causing HIV infection, ARC, AIDS and ultimately death has the strong emotional connotation of mother nature, God, turning against her children through the immune system that she created in the first place to protect us. The other parallel is on the level of group dynamics. The convenor was the 'mother' who created the seven experiential groups—i.e., her 'children'—but she was also responsible for the non-fishbowl. The more cohesive the latter became, the more it felt as if the convenor was 'killing' her first seven children.

All this has to do with the group unconscious and the nature of properly conducted experiential groups. Such groups are purposefully created psychological spaces in which intense interaction between virtual strangers can take place within a very short time. The individuals become a group as a whole with its particular 'culture' and group unconscious that bonds them together on a deep level. This rapid group cohesion is possible because each individual's unconscious part is in primary contact with the unconscious parts of the others, ready to respond, react to or merge with each other. The representatives came to the non-fishbowl as members of their respective groups, but as the interaction intensified, the group in the here-and-now developed and thus started threatening the existence of the previous seven small groups. Some refused to be disloyal and clung emotionally to their old group, rejecting the emerging new cohesion ('I wouldn't dream of disclosing anything about my group.' 'I feel supported by members of my group watching us silently in the audience'). On an unconscious level members were torn by the opposing forces of being part of two groups, one dispersed, i.e., 'dying', in the silent audience and the other coming alive in the centre. The result of the struggle was enormous tension and anxiety.

The only constructive solution to this tension between two small groups was to transcend the struggle of having to belong to either of them and start experiencing the workshop as a whole as the space for togetherness. Perhaps this is what another group analyst detected when she observed that the various parts of the workshop had become inverted. According to CR, in the large setting of the plenary sessions people experienced the intimacy and support usually offered within small groups.

The third comment was by JG. She stated that the non-fishbowl 'actually served to contain the kind of acting out that is so frequent in AIDS workshops by translating the underlying primitive reactions (mostly fear and rage) into verbal symbolisms.' On this point several group conductors and others seem to agree.

In retrospect it can be said that the non-fishbowl provided a focal point to the workshop in which the deep unconscious, unspeakable reactions of primordial panic and rage and the phenomenon of splitting became accessible to exploration within, through and by the groups.

CHAPTER NINE

What happened behind seven closed doors?

As the reader must be aware by now, the workshop had been divided into small experiential groups earlier on. They had a first meeting before the non-fishbowl session and another afterwards. In the following these small groups are described.

Composition of the small groups

Much thought was given to balancing the seven experiential groups. They were composed in accordance with the information received through the registration forms as well as my personal knowledge of a number of participants.

The criteria, in order of priority, were:

1. working place: those working together were put in different groups
2. sexes: 3–4 men in each group
3. HIV/AIDS programme experience: 5–6 or more members with considerable experience in each group

4. group analysts: 1–2 in each group
5. medical doctors: 1–3 in each group
6. other primary care workers: 4–5 in each group
7. avoid accumulation of any characteristic in any group
8. avoid any individual being alone with a relevant characteristic not shared by anyone else in the group.

The aim was to ensure sufficient heterogeneity for
dynamic interaction to take place in each group. At the same
time we tried to anticipate and eliminate possible sources of
conflict extraneous to the theme of the workshop. People
working in the same programme or institution were sep-
arated into various groups, so as to offer them a safer
environment in which to talk about their feelings. Also it
was hoped that in this way a refreshingly greater variety of
individual experiences would be brought back into the work
situation. As far as it could be foreseen, we attempted to
identify and put in different groups persons who for whatever reason would not feel comfortable in each others' com-
pany or might clash with each other. The intention was to
avoid adding interpersonal difficulties to the already explo-
sive topic of the workshop. A special effort was put into
working out the likely relationship between the conductor
and the group as a whole, as well as to making sure that there
would be no serious incompatibilities between the conductor
and any one member within the group.

However, not everything could be foreseen. Due to last-
minute cancellations and the total number of drop-outs,
some decisions about replacements and additions had to be
made in a hurry and without sufficient information or time
to think them through. In one group a participant found
himself with an ex-fellow student being the group conductor.
It was an uneasy situation for which I apologized after the
workshop. A male participant felt isolated and rather alone,
being the only gay member of his group due to a drop-out. In
another group two members' strong personalities and firmly
held contrasting attitudes led to a gladiatorial contest
between them, thus frustrating the others and hampering
the otherwise excellent work of the group as a whole.

Thus, despite all efforts, the meticulously thought-out composition could not be maintained. It had to be revised several times and towards the end in a hurried fashion. The greatest distortion occurred in the group in which out of nine participants expected only five turned up on the day. Table 1 shows the composition of the groups before and after these distortions.

Careful consideration was also given to the allocation of rooms. The convenor (AM) and one of the co-convenors (JB) did not participate in the small groups, which left them slightly envious and rather sad. They, together with the administrator (BL), had to deal with various back-up mat-

Table 1

	HIV/AIDS experience								
Groups	1	2	3	total	F	M	GA	MD	pcw
I	6 (6)	2 (1)	2 (2)	10 (9)	6 (6)	4 (3)	1 (1)	1 (1)	5
II	5 (5)	2 (2)	2 (3)	9 (10)	6 (7)	3 (3)	1 (2)	2 (2)	5
III	6 (6)	3 (3)	–	9 (9)	6 (6)	3 (3)	2 (2)	1 (1)	5
IV	5 (6)	2 (4)	–	7 (10)	5 (7)	2 (3)	1 (2)	1 (1)	3
V	5 (5)	2 (2)	2 (2)	9 (9)	5 (6)	4 (3)	2 (2)	2 (2)	4
VI	4 (8)	–	2 (2)	66 (10)	4 (7)	2 (3)	2 (2)	3 (3)	1
VII	5 (6)	2 (2)	1 (2)	8 (10)	5 (7)	3 (3)	2 (2)	1 (1)	4
total	36	13	9	58	37	21	11	11	27
Workshop									
JB	–	–	1	1	1	–	1	1	–
AM	–	1	–	1	1	–	1	–	–
total	36	14	10	60	39	21	13	12	27

"HIV/AIDS experience" means direct experience/knowledge of HIV/AIDS-related programmes, "1" being a lot, "2" some and "3" very little or none. F = female; M = male; GA = group analyst; MD = physician; pcw = primary care worker (other than medical doctor). The first figures represent the actual membership of the groups. The figures in brackets indicate the composition as originally planned.

ters while the small groups were in session. All others, including the speakers and the chairman, took part in the small group experience.

Before the coffee break at 10:50, JB explained to the workshop the criteria used to form the groups and the painstaking work that went into it. She expressed the hope that participants would find the composition of the groups acceptable or at least tolerable.

The nature of the reports

In the following we give those glimpses into each group that appear in participants' responses to the evaluation form (appendix VI) and some, partly very extensive, reports by the group conductors and others. It has to be borne in mind that no specific question was asked about the small experiential groups in the evaluation form. Therefore, every feedback is entirely spontaneous.

The reports cover the contents of the group discussion, descriptions of the group process and interactions and interpretations of both. Each report has a very personal flavour and is thoroughly sincere and valid from the point of view of the person who wrote it. However, it is not necessarily reflecting what the others experienced in the group. It will be noted that in the comments appearing at the end of each report participants sometimes describe very different and even contrasting feelings, thoughts and impressions about the same group. Although it might strike one as surprising, such divergence of views simply reflects the wide variety of subjective experiences and is not unusual in this type of groups.

The amount of feedback varies, depending on how many members of each group replied and how long each reply was. Although it is tempting to do so, it would be wrong to take the total length of each description as a measure of how successful or emotionally engaging the particular group was. In one case, at least, the contrary holds: because the group seems to have achieved considerable intimacy and depth, members as well as the conductor found it rather difficult to talk about their experience in detail.

Editing was mainly aimed at ensuring anonymity and discretion. In order not to breach confidentiality, various devices were used to disguise the identity of participants, such as changing names and the original numeration of the groups, and in a few cases reversing the genders and keeping direct quotations anonymous. As mentioned in the introduction, with a few exceptions, 'she' is used when referring to the conductor of a group and 'he' when referring to a group member. No distinction is made between reports written by group members or the conductor, and the latter is always referred to in the third person. Great care has been taken not to distort the meaning and balance of positive and negative statements.

Reports by group members and conductors

Group I

At the start of the first small group session some of us attempted to express our own fears and panic that had been awakened during the preceding talks. One or two individuals owned that they felt scared of AIDS for their loved ones, but the group as a whole was determined to put aside and ignore the fears and the panic. We all agreed that we had both personal and professional reasons for being here.

As the group tentatively unfolded into life, it became clear that we were profoundly concerned with wanting to feel more secure, to take charge of those issues that threatened to overwhelm us. The language we used became esoteric and exclusive. We lurched into a debate about facts and figures, the language of bigotry, other people's attitudes, the politics of AIDS, and we compared the systems of hospitals and countries. We became more and more globally fixated.

While our intellectual resources were being challenged to provide certainty and answers, we tried repeatedly to get back to the uncertainty that lay behind all this. We couldn't very well. We talked of our fear of dying and especially of dying out of control. Is it the way you die or the way you live that matters? How does one endure the unendurable? Then, more facts and figures. I felt isolated, like a very sick patient without a voice. Somebody asked again, who are the experts who can be trusted? A doctor said that he finds himself trusted because he listens to the patient. I wondered how on earth could we start listening to the 'patient' in this group? The members expressed some frustration and anger at not being able to reach each other. Some of us felt attacked and taken over by those who were more verbal in the exchange of opinions and certainties. A member said: 'All this certainty makes me feel very uneasy'. I thought he might have chosen the word 'dis-eased' for on the symbolic level it amounts to the same thing. Then the conductor announced the end of the session. I exclaimed with a feeling of disappointment, 'Is it already time?' It seemed to me to be over awfully quickly. Like a very short life.

In the afternoon we focussed on death. We attempted to express to each other how we might feel if we had AIDS. Some would feel guilty, others ashamed and disgusted, someone else terrified and revengeful: we all resonated to the horror of loneliness and suffering, of going mad and maybe dying without dignity. The lover of an AIDS patient had committed suicide. One doctor among us felt guilty for not having saved him from his act of self-destruction. Remembering the talk about bigotry and loathing for some AIDS sufferers, I said that if I had AIDS I think I'd be scared I might die (inwardly) of hatred first. The others asked, 'Whose hatred, your own or other people's?' But it didn't seem to make any difference.

Our conductor asked us how many of us could be sure that we would survive tonight? Two people said emphatically that they knew without doubt they were not going to die tonight. We then side-stepped directly talking about our own deaths by asking one of the doctors to tell us how AIDS patients face death. He explained that people swing between denial and acceptance of what is going to happen to them— just as we were now doing in the group, it seemed to me. Some people fight so hard that they win a little more time for themselves. Others despair and die very quickly.

Someone talked of a recent bereavement and claimed to have coped with that by remaining in control of everything that could be controlled. This would be the way that he would face his own death. We realized how important it is to find a meaning in life, even when, maybe especially when in the process of dying. Or maybe especially here-and-now, in the group and out there.

As in the morning, a dynamic developed whereby the 'experts' dominated the discussion with their comprehensive knowledge, sharing their experiences and comparing theories. But the group felt that this became too competitive, and somehow we were all alienated once again.

The conductor tried several times to facilitate a discussion about sexuality and intimacy. She asked: 'In the light of all this information, who would now change their sexual practices?' She wants us to talk about our own deaths, and now about our sexual practices? What kind of group is this? We've only just met. It's too soon to be close. It's too soon to die. Can we trust the prophylactic efficiency of our conductor?

No, not yet. This group lived vibrantly, but cautiously. We were preoccupied with fear of annihilation, split off from our own destructive feelings, longing for a full, rich and intimate contact, but too scared of death to start. In my opinion it was a celibate group. I wonder, if we had lived a little longer, might we, could we, would we have dared to make love?

* * *

'I was irritated in the small group by a member who arrived late and put forward his own views in a very didactic way. He monopolized the group's time in an insensitive fashion. Being only a newly formed group, I think we probably could not have—comfortably—dealt with this disturbance in a much more effective way. I regret that it happened. Without it we might have had an even more interesting and productive session.'

'Our group didn't work especially well—perhaps because no confidentiality contract was made at the outset. We got on better when we all personally explored our fears about AIDS.'

'. . . and of course the small groups are always interesting and stimulating . . .'

Group II

Nobody was missing as we started. The conductor said that we were to exchange our thoughts and feelings about the talks and our own experience of working in the field of AIDS. Members introduced themselves and said briefly why they had come to the workshop. Difficulties with distance from and closeness to people affected by HIV/AIDS were discussed. How does one cope with it all? One particular member, let us call her Viv, jumped in full of 'good news' and interesting facts. She told us how to emphasize the positive. Ignoring her advice, several members recounted sombre experiences, all underscoring the shame of AIDS and the awfulness of death. The body was merely bundled into a black plastic bag, and the relatives were not allowed to see it. This was spoken of so movingly that some in the group were near to tears. Again Viv rushed in with more up-to-date, helpful information. However, the group stopped her from further pep talks, at least for the time being.

An AIDS educator said that it was like the phoney war: they had lots of trained people, but no patients to practise on. This left the workers feeling frustrated and also made them anxious about how it will be when patients do eventually appear.

A worker from a drug addiction unit spoke of his bloody frustration with some drug users' destructiveness: though they are antibody positive, they carry on seeking sexual contacts with people who attend the clinic and have not yet been infected with HIV. These two groups seem to fall for each other. The worker is left with a dreadful feeling of impotence. As the theme of impotence and helplessness was taken up, Viv suggested vigorous physical exercise as a remedy against frustration.

The need for a support network was mentioned. One cannot unload these feelings at home. Some relief can be found in sharing them with fellow workers. On the other hand, in one's own institution it is not always safe to tell colleagues about your feelings. Today's workshop was one thing, but where is the on-going help? Viv admitted that patients do get under her skin at times. There is the problem of burn-out, stress, then one withdraws. Several members spoke of the various techniques they use to protect themselves because they feel so stressed. The talk moved on to 'Are we forgotten as workers?' 'Do the bosses, the community and society really know what we are putting up with?'

A few minutes before the end of the morning session the fishbowl was mentioned, and a member volunteered to represent our group. He checked out with the group the sort of things that he would say, and then we broke up for lunch.

After the fishbowl the group's work became more intense than it had been in the morning session. We started with our fishbowl representative telling us about his experience. He had really been in the hot seat and had had no idea that it would feel like that. He complained that he had been misled. To the conductor's question whether he felt she had dropped him into it, the answer was yes and he was angry with her for it. After a while he admitted that the experience had not been all negative. On the contrary, it had been very powerful. He had learned a lot about himself, observing his own internal reactions.

AIDS patients get everything, all the resources. Other ill people need these resources, and why should there be such a demandingness coming from the AIDS patients? A lot of rivalry is stirred up at the way the AIDS patients demand and get. Anger at their position of specialness was explored. Why do we lean over backwards to be so accomodating? Yet, it was very difficult to withstand it and say 'no' to AIDS patients.

The theme recurred that education was not enough, people know the facts but do not act on them. Why do people go on having dangerous sex? Someone suggested it was Russian roulette, you want to take the risk and have the excitement. Another member said he would try to protect his daughter, tell her about AIDS, but he was worried. Others too thought of their nearest and dearest. It was very frightening to think about them in connection with AIDS. When it came down to it, would I be able to go on being caring? Suppose I had a boy of six who was in the playground with another boy of the same age who was HIV-infected? Would I really want my child to be a close friend or even be in the same school with that child? The group struggled with their feelings, trying to be honest. A number of them gave up by saying it was difficult to envisage how one would feel until one was actually in the situation. Once the experience hits, who knows what one might do.

One of the women whose son is gay, and possibly promiscuous, told the group about her anxieties. The AIDS educator resonated by saying that it was not easy to be known as someone working with AIDS patients. Another group member said that AIDS could not be pushed away, and there is so much uncertainty about it. Viv was quick to offer definite information. The conductor intervened, saying that we needed to stay with the feelings for a few moments rather than rush into the facts. The group returned to struggle with the difficult feelings: it is unpleasant to be called the 'AIDS-lady' and it is hard to live with the anxiety of whether one's son would continue to put himself at risk by his lifestyle. Being available, being there, was the most important thing, someone said. It wasn't always doing. Activity was seen as a defence against being there. Activity could be nothing but imposing on someone your own need to help.

An educator talked about his work with nurses. He was teaching them how they must deal with AIDS patients. Some of the nurses were horrified, saying they did not want to wear gloves, as it went against the grain of doing good nursing. Another member said how important it was to be in contact with the messy bits.

Viv started talking about condoms; how essential it was to inform everyone in the family about their correct use. There was no response. After a while a thoughtful member said that it was not just giving information. It was the whole issue of sensitivity of relationships and relating. The group expressed a need to be with somebody close to love and to touch, which led to the question: Can you be trustful? There was a comparison made between sex as a fusion, a warm and loving experience, and sex as a purely mechanical screwing, a wham, bam, bang sort of experience which made aloneness more unbearable. The group wondered if AIDS tests us as people, our humanity, our honesty and puts our mutual interdependence very much on the line.

There was a minute or two before our next task of saying goodbye and going on to have tea. We broke up the group reluctantly.

* * *

'The small group was a good experience. Most of us were very much in touch with our feelings, contributed our experience and responded to each other. The group even managed to contain one particularly anxious lady who tended to block the expression of fear and feelings of sadness or uncertainty.'

'The small group was quite a struggle, I think due to professional rivalry and the kind of "preciousness" of the area that CF described in his talk. I found myself oscillating between hope and despair.'

'I found the group work hard. We had only one day, and there was so much to discuss. The silences were uncomfortable. I felt it was wasted time when the issues were so enormous and complex. I know silences are part of an ongoing group, but they only annoyed me since I knew we'd not be meeting again. I wanted to get on with it. It became too much a "head" thing and not a "heart" experience.'

'I didn't find the small groups very useful except at a shallow level of sharing. I suppose I expected more direction, more equal sharing of how things were for us as workers, as opposed to "free" participation; more encouragement to let the pain, confusion and discomfort out and end on a positive, affirmative, empowering note.'

Group III

At first there was an 'all at sea' feeling in the group. Members seemed to be preoccupied with the power of society and were wondering how one could retain a coherent sense of self. Some described how they found themselves quite unconsciously conforming to the new guidelines. They had settled into monogamous relationships or identified with the aggressor and turned their back on liberal attitudes that had once been important to them. The worry was expressed that those liberal attitudes might destroy or damage the world the children of today were going to live in. The parents were at a loss to know what they would say to their children. Sex which they had experienced with fear of producing life now carried fear of producing death.

The group tried to wrestle with the dilemma of the personal in conflict with something bigger—a group of individuals 'all at sea', sharing our mortality, wanting to find in one another some strength to cope with the battering we were taking. There were feelings of despondency. If no one can understand, perhaps it is better to stay alone and each struggle in our own way. There was a brief hope that individual psychotherapy could analyse the difficulties away, but this gave way to a more reassuring idea that we did not have to strive to be completely sorted out, rather to be able to survive uncertainty.

Perhaps the nearest we came to putting these very primitive, nameless feelings and fears into words was towards the end of the afternoon session (after the fishbowl). The anger that had been permeating the group was articulated then quite clearly as rage. The group seemed to demand that the conductor deal with it by taking it on herself, thereby relieving the group's feelings. Her refusal to do so enraged the group further but served to acknowledge the violence of the feelings and the need to find other ways of dealing with them than simply absorbing them, as is tempting to do with people in distress.

Not getting round to the real issues and, indeed, not knowing what the real issues are, were clearly problems in the hospitals and health education. The concrete nature of much of the content of the discussion in the group is perhaps not so surprising, given that the feelings we were struggling with were inevitably located mostly in the paranoid–schizoid realm.

There had been some concern expressed about what the GAS/IGA felt about AIDS and whether it was a homophobic society. Again, this was partly projection, partly uncertainty about historical analytic attitudes and partly locating the IGA/GAS with the rest of society, which was perceived as not understanding.'

* * *

'My small group experience was positive.'

'It was good to be part of a group and for once not have to carry the responsibility for organizing it. . . .'

'No contract of confidentiality was established in our group. As most members of such a workshop have no previous experience of group analysis, in my opinion the conductor needs to establish the rules (if the group does not do this for itself). I think we all found the small group very useful.'

'I found the small group frustrating. I wanted to explore and share feelings whilst others in the group were only willing to share thinking.'

Group IV

The morning session began with someone expressing his anger and feeling of helplessness vis-à-vis drug users who inject themselves, knowing the risk of possible HIV infection they take. Other group members resonated and identified with such behaviour: they have been sexually involved with more than one partner without taking the necessary precautions. It was admirable how quickly these group members sought to get inside the skin of their own experiences and difficulties with their clients. Hitherto denied fears were put into words and led on to anger against certain groups and society for labelling people. It was pointed out that splitting and projection were at the root of labelling and discrimination.

Both commiseration and envy were expressed towards the person who chose to represent the group in the 'fishbowl'. He talked about his need to control what information went out from the group. He also thought it was expected of him as a male group member to represent the group. The male/female issue, difference and damage, then flared up briefly but was not pursued.

At the start of the afternoon session anger against the IGA was expressed: it was not possible to present the small

group's experience in the fishbowl! The question of boundaries was explored. If clients and workers are included
within a 'family' boundary, as it were, how will that affect
them? Some group members felt alarmed and threatened by
the extent to which other workers had become involved in
the lives of their clients dying of AIDS. Questions of how to
inform clients of their condition and how to deal with their
fears and one's own fears were discussed in relation to the
setting of boundaries. Someone talked about issues of power
between client and worker and about her own manipulation
of her family when she was chronically sick as a child.

It was mentioned that some clients with AIDS appear to
transcend their illness, grow and become outwardly directed,
open to others. On the other hand, many workers experience
panic and exhaustion, especially when faced with clients
who become brain-damaged. The worker might be left with a
sense of futility about his/her own efforts and life. How long
could one continue coping with clients' altered personalities
and with clients and friends dying? By contrast, the possibility of burn-out and feelings of uselessness seemed new
for some workers.

Members of the group expressed fear at how they themselves would cope with contracting HIV infection and AIDS
and deal with their relations and loved ones. The group
wound itself into the areas of loss, depression, despair and
hopelessness in their work and themselves. We talked about
burn-out, how to remain competent and loving, calm, giving,
outgoing; how to manage in the face of such continuous
change and movement towards death in young people. The
existential issues, birth in death and transcendence, were
touched upon near the end of the group, but not explored.

* * *

Note: Several members of this group remarked spontaneously on the evaluation form that the small group
experience was 'useful', 'positive', without expanding on
their statement. One lamented the lack of time for another

small group session. No one had anything negative to say about this group.

Group V

After some initial flights from the personal, the conductor drew to the group's attention that we were talking as if we were the only ones who were concerned, who knew about the topic and who worked with HIV, ARC and AIDS. Immediately the group delved into the solitude of dying. Some of the group members seemed to have a need to hold on to this loneliness and isolation. All this paralleled that clinging onto the AIDS field and reluctance to allow outsiders to join in that had been mentioned by AM in her talk.

During the interval between the first and the second session, when there was no one in the room, the centre table was removed by a person unknown. The conductor logged this little piece of surreptitious acting out in her mind but quickly forgot it as the group moved on. No one mentioned it, no one owned up to having removed the table. The event remained unanalysed.

In the second session (after the fishbowl), the group talked with one member who was angry because promiscuity was attributed to him and other gay men. He blamed society's general attitude. Promiscuity was then assessed in other terms, such as need of physical intimacy, fear of emotional dependence.

For a few moments the conductor had a sense that this was a side-track. She then braced herself and said: 'The group may feel that we have been invited to be promiscuous, to get into an intimate and revealing situation with each other when there is so little time left.' Except for one person, everyone was surprised at her words. 'Where did that come from?' asked someone rather scornfully. Another member wondered whether the rejection of that interpretation was not an attack on the conductor herself because of the swift opening and sudden ending of the group. He himself felt angry about the death of the group.

The fact that the centre table's removal was never analysed appeared to be symbolic. It contributed to the general sense of uncertainty. A stable feature of the circle could be taken away in a stealthy, anarchic way while the group as a whole colluded with the perpetrator by moving on fast and luring the conductor to forget the incident.

Sensitivity and feelings surrounding homosexuality were very much around and were touched upon, but there was not enough time and trust to address them in depth.

* * *

'During the last group session there was a great sense of "optimism" amongst us. Things were bad, yes, but not as bad as they seemed, and if we only worked together we may be able to change things. . . . I had the overwhelming feeling (which I shared with the group) that this optimism was false. I am sure this is partly due to my personal distress while counselling HIV-positive people and AIDS patients and seeing so many of them die. However, I feel that excessively positive thinking can be dangerous.'

'The small group experiences were open and caring and I recognized even more clearly my own need for an ongoing support group!'

'I felt less uncomfortable and more confident in my small group than I thought I would. Would I be able to deal with it? Fears of HIV, dying . . . may be one thing, fears of group work are quite another. I found the small group work useful.'

Group VI

I was taken aback by two people not appearing. That was in addition to the two cancellations, about which we knew already. We were left with six survivors, which made for quite an intimate group. We talked about institutional resistances to the development of HIV/AIDS work and programmes as well as our personal responses to the opening papers.

In the afternoon after the fishbowl murderous and revengeful feelings among HIV-positive patients towards those unconsciously held 'to blame' for their predicament were discussed.

* * *

'The small group I was in felt good to me. Someone spoke of his own experiences of trying to run a staff group with people of very different professions who all happened to have dealings with the same patients. He said that he had been unable to hold the group together. I was astonished at the relief that I felt. I am currently attempting to run several staff groups and feel very unskilled in the management of at least one of them, which is a meeting once a month for anybody who works in any capacity with people with HIV infection. We may have six or twenty-six in this group. They may be priests, social workers, psychiatrists, nurses, or volunteers from the local helpline. I have deliberately made it as open as possible and put no pressure on anybody to attend more often than they wish. It actually works quite well, but I always feel afterwards that I have walked across Niagara on a tightrope with my eyes closed. For reasons I cannot begin to fathom, this group member telling us about his own lack of success with a similarly assorted group gave me a great sense of liberation. Perhaps the example of a noble failure released me from my own pressure to succeed. Whatever it was, I don't run the group any differently than before but I no longer worry about it as much as I did. So, thank you for that!'

'There was the inevitable debate about the analytic views on homosexuality and whether or not aggression was expressed in anal sexual activity.' However, the obsession of some heterosexual people with, and their phantasies about anal sexuality among gay men can also be aggressive. A group member felt that such discussions were 'reminiscent of the way the Jews were talked about in Germany in the 1930s and 1940s'. His strong feelings brought home to another group member how very lonely it must be to be a gay man, AIDS or not, in a society firmly holding the notion of homosexuality as being a perversion of the truth and health of hetero-sexuality.'

Group VII

The talk in the morning session remained stuck on the factual level. Each member introduced himself, and those with personal experience of working with AIDS patients held the floor for some time. We needed quite a long time before one member felt it safe to express her disappointment, having hoped that there would be more space for expressing feelings. Again and again we came back to facts. The two empty chairs were never removed, neither did anyone men-tion them, though they were disturbing. The absence of those two members underlined the ambivalence.

The second session (after the fishbowl) was productive. We had reconstituted the circle without the empty chairs and made it smaller, which undoubtedly helped. Feelings about death were discussed. Some personal disclosure helped to make the group feel more intimate. We were now able to acknowledge the positive presence of two members who coin-cidentally, after booking the workshop, had had to face acute family problems that might well have stopped them from coming. Did the fishbowl experience also help? Envy was expressed of other groups who had reported spontaneous intimacy (or was it only mock-intimacy?). The feeling was that, excellent as the morning presentations had been, our experiential group had only just really started, and more time could have been put to good use.

* * *

'In "my" group, there seemed to be no ground rules of confidentiality or aims. I felt little trust and support. Maybe it was due to a woman who would not stop talking, showing off and intellectualizing.'

'Groups seem to yield unexpected personal experiences. . . . There was a woman in my group whose recent experience with suicide and her capacity to talk about it enabled me to articulate my anger at suicide, death in general and the AIDS virus in particular. Which led to the sorrow of it, having to live with it. . . .'

'I was chosen by my group to be a member of the "fishbowl" and reluctantly filled the role. Having been involved with death in my family at the time of the workshop, I was in touch with my inner world, which I believe contributed to my being chosen. However, when they chose me my group members were unaware of my bereavement.' [Note: it must be linked with this participant's experience in the small group and the 'fishbowl' that she gave a very positive evaluation of the workshop as a whole!]

'The unexpected personal experience for me was to see the great difficulty I have in coping with separation. In my small group we explored the impact the death of AIDS sufferers has on their relatives. While this was going on, I realized how intolerable it is for me to leave my family, particularly my seven-year-old daughter, whenever I have to go to work away from home. As a result of this experience I intend to seek group therapy to resolve my difficulties. Thank you.'

A group-analytic overview of the seven groups

It is impossible for an outsider like the author to know and to convey what exactly happened in an experiential small group behind a closed door. Even those who were in that room can give no more than glimpses of their experience. There is no way they or others can re-live it. Nevertheless, the reports and feedback by participants and group conductors as well as comparison with other experiential and staff support groups dealing with HIV/AIDS give enough evidence to substantiate the following observations.

The total situation that constituted the background to these seven groups has to be kept in mind at all times if we want to understand what went on in them. The salient aspects of the total situation were the workshop's theme and objectives as stated in the leaflet announcing it (appendix I), the type of participants it had attracted, the institution in which the workshop took place and, last but not least, the four speakers' personalities and styles, their thoughts, ideas and feelings (chapter 7) to which participants had been exposed before breaking up into small groups. The second small group session was affected by everything that preceded it, especially the non-fishbowl (chapter 8) and the general atmosphere that developed during the lunch break (chapter 6).

Virtually all seven groups started with some ideas touched upon in the talks preceding the first small group session. Also, the presence of one or the other speaker as a group member created a particular dynamic in three of the groups. It is understandable that the group would consider the speaker as the local guru on the theme of his talk and spend some time preoccupied with asking him questions and receiving his answers. Unavoidably, he would be seen as a special member of the group, and a triangle between him, the others and the group conductor would crystallize. The latter would have the not so easy task of shifting this triangle so that the group did not remain bogged down in it. A strong, opposing or antagonistic individual might emerge, who challenges the specialness of the guru. The verbal fight between the two might reduce the group and its conductor 'to the role of a Greek Goddess'. The contest might become 'too mesmerizing for the group to escape: to turn one's back on the battle might mean to miss the special current interaction.'

Predictably, there was initial resistance to dealing with the issues on an emotional level. Given the brevity of time, it was up to the conductor to take the initiative and push the group through the barrier of defensive occupations—such as mere factual information exchange, intellectual discussions and side-tracking into sex-talk—towards an in-depth exploration of the more painful and frightening aspects of the AIDS crisis.

Offering information, discussing facts and figures, is a defence against uncertainty and helplessness that appears regularly in groups dealing with HIV/AIDS. Our groups managed to overcome it and talk overtly about these unsettling feelings. Group III found reassurance in the wise thought that 'we did not have to strive to be completely sorted out, rather to be able to survive uncertainty.'

Sex can be a genuine subject for discussion, closely connected with HIV/AIDS. However, very often under the sex theme there are other, more difficult issues. Anal sex, promiscuity and homophobia were mentioned and debated. The force of passion behind some of the verbal exchanges indicated the fear of not being acceptable, the rage about the anticipated rejection and the determination to assert oneself against all odds. A group conductor wrote: 'Homophobia was a major issue which could easily occupy a similar workshop. One wonders about the nature of liberal attitudes in society and how much more persecutory society could become if AIDS continues to spread out of our control. Perhaps what we were trying to talk about during much of the day was self-preservation, in both literal and psychological terms, and the guilt associated with survival.'

One of the frequent defences appearing in groups that deal with HIV/AIDS is the manic defence, the inability to stay with sadness and pain, the compulsive need to go on, to act and to be jolly. Sometimes it is unstoppable, collective, hysterical laughter. It can appear all of a sudden, like a switch-off from heavy gloom. This did not seem to have happened in any of these groups, but there were pointers in that direction.

When the manic defence is in operation, sex can be a welcome subject for banter and cracking jokes, to vitalize and shock—in other words, to get away as far as possible from the darkness of death and dying—except that with HIV/AIDS the escape route of cheerful sex leads back to death. The suggestion of condoms on the Christmas tree for one's adolescent children becomes a loving gesture and cause for hearty laughter for one person, while those in the group who refuse to collude with the manic defence might find it a chilling and macabre imagery.

Another manifestation of resistance is the avoidance of the here-and-now in favour of the 'out there'. For some reason, whenever groups deal with HIV/AIDS, it is harder to recognize and vanquish this defence, which is so familiar to all group analysts and, indeed, all psychodynamically trained psychotherapists. For instance, in one of the small groups, someone expressed his anxiety for being alone as a gay man in the workshop. This statement astounded the group, since everyone else had the impression that the majority of male participants in the workshop were gay. What neither he himself nor the others in the group recognized was that he was actually talking about his isolation in the here-and-now, being the only gay man in the small group itself. In another group, the question of who were the experts who could be trusted in the AIDS field was raised repeatedly. No one noticed the obvious: the group unconscious was querying the trustworthiness of the experts in the here-and-now, within the group, who were undermining each other's credibility. The resistance to looking at and dealing with feelings in the here-and-now appeared under another form when members of Group II said that 'it is difficult to envisage how one would feel until one is actually in the situation.'

Undoubtedly, the most distressing subject is one's own existence or, even worse, the integrity of the self being threatened. Sex-talk might be used to avoid having to face the issue of one's own death. When groups start talking about it, a last ditch of resistance might come into operation—the defence mechanism of isolation. The group is talking about the very things that truly matter at that moment, but without the concomitant feelings being expressed or even experienced. The result is a weird sensation of unreality, reported in different words. 'People were able to talk movingly about themselves and their concerns but (failed in their attempt to address) the very primitive nameless feelings and fears, which they guessed underlay them. This produced the strange feeling of knowing you were communicating but in an autistic way, not reaching what we needed to discuss.' Of course, what is repressed at one point in time appears later. Someone reported after the workshop: 'I feel flat, not depressed at all, surprisingly untouched by the day at this point. A couple of days after writing this, I awoke, startled, in the middle of the night and then became restless. I suddenly had the panicky thought that I was HIV positive and became very concerned. This worry only died away after a week or so.'

It is surely connected with the powerful primitive feelings when they remain unspoken and unspeakable and the equally powerful defences against them that the conductor might feel helplessly reduced to impotent frustration. It is as if she were scanning with her eyes a massive wall with various entrances that one after the other turn out to be painted on solid stone as soon as she approaches them. The group conductor might feel unsure of herself, doubt the appropriateness of her own interventions or non-intervention and wonder why on earth she has accepted this task in the first place. Two conductors reported having felt de-skilled at times, others were left with the frustration that their group had not reached the depths they would have wished for.

From a group-analytic point of view one of the most interesting aspects is how the basic feelings and themes that appear in the unconscious of every group connect up with anxieties and emotions around HIV/AIDS. For instance, there is the question of trust, which arises in the early life of any group. The unspoken questions are: Can I trust this group? How close can I let this group come to me? Is it alright to be intimate? Can we fuse, be fertile and creative together? Is it safe or will I get hurt? The same questions could be asked in this post-AIDS world by any young person tentatively approaching a potential lover. The attention is called to this parallel in the account of Group I. Moreover, AIDS seems to threaten our basic trust in society, nature and life itself (chapter 1).

Some participants alleged having been restricted in the expression of their feelings because no rules of confidentiality had been given. It is true that rules of confidentiality had not been spelt out, but this default became a welcome excuse to resist going too deeply into painful and distressing areas in the small groups. In fact, there was, surprisingly, a great openness and spontaneity in the plenary session, where there was no guarantee of confidentiality whatsoever and the tape-recorder was running.

Another theme that links group phenomena and HIV/AIDS is the issue of blurred boundaries and role confusion. The one mentioned already—a speaker or expert being both a group member, 'one of us', an equal—-mirrored the situation in certain specialized clinics where some nurses or doctors (i.e., the experts) are HIV positive or have developed AIDS and from time to time become patients (i.e., are treated the same as others on the ward, as 'one of us').

Another parallel with the ward situation was discovered by Group III: 'The problem of the doctor knowing his patient so well, that he is less able to be available to him when he is dying, was manifested in the group through the conductor knowing one of the participants well. . . . Mutual expression of anger and regret seemed to shift some of the heaviness but stimulated resentment in other members about having to deal with personal relationships. This parallels the ward situation.'

Perhaps the most obvious link between group-related and AIDS-related emotional issues is the idea of ending. In the

natural sequence of emotions one of the reactions to immi-
nent death is to be angry and fight it. Groups protest vehe-
mently at times against their ending. There have been
numerous remarks by participants about the shortness of the
experiential groups in this workshop. Some of these reactions had to do with the reluctance to accept the death of their
respective groups. Obviously, 'three or even four sessions
would have allowed much more work to be done'. On the
other hand, as a group analyst pointed out, 'the total time
available influences the way time is used'. A sharply defined,
short period might concentrate the minds on the relevant
issues, while a longer time, if not well managed, can be spent
on defensive talk. In my experience with this and similar
workshops, protests about the length of time always appear
one way or the other.

It seems that after the non-fishbowl experience there was a
shift, or at least a noticeable change, in some groups. Reports
indicate an increased ability in the groups to express feelings, especially anger in the here-and-now, talk about painful personal experiences in an atmosphere of increased
intimacy. One of the group conductors reported that the
mood was 'low-key and appropriately depressed'.

What was also helpful about the small groups was simply
the space in which to talk and express emotions. Some participants succeeded in using this opportunity more than
others. As a result, the latter found their small groups
'quite a struggle' and frustration, whilst the former found
them rewarding and worthwhile. Several expressed heartfelt
thanks for the group experience and for what they got out of
it on a personal level.

CHAPTER TEN

Facing the darkness in the last plenary session

Summary

by Sarah T. Willis

Most people felt it had been very valuable to be part of something that is dynamic and moving. They enjoyed meeting people from other disciplines—Yes, we would like to have more workshops, or a short, intensive course. Maybe we could also become a clearinghouse for information about support groups across the country. Somebody suggested the AIDS issue be dealt with in large groups. The ambition of this surprised me when I thought of the primitive forces unleashed in such a setting—but, who knows, maybe this would be just the place to look at the strong feelings around AIDS?

Two comments were made that I found very interesting. The first suggested that role-play might be used to help us to understand what it's like, for example, to be a member of the family of an AIDS sufferer. The second comment seemed to contain a complaint that we could never really change unless we could meet a person with AIDS. After all, young people who had been confronted by someone with AIDS had experienced a kind of transformation in their attitudes. I thought these were interesting comments, because they seemed to contain a denial of what had actually occurred here today, even if on the symbolic level. We had come powerfully face to face with the virus and its consequences. We had embarked on a kind of role-play, or 'drama', in the fishbowl. In the second session of my small group someone said that she, too, had been momentarily shocked by the belief that someone in the central circle really had AIDS. I think these two comments also point the way to the role of group analysis in this issue. In facing the AIDS crisis, the tension created by primitive internal and devastating external reality can only be alleviated by the existence of an intermediate area of experience, Winnicott's notion of the transitional object, applied to the group.

A few key-themes from the day re-emerged. Who are the victims, those who die or those who are left? Or, I thought to myself, all of us, in the sense that we find it so difficult to stay with our sense of weakness and vulnerability? We noticed that we had been exploring how to contain the hostility. Much of the day's imagery had been connected with warring primitives: darts, blow-pipes, victims and savages. AM brought these themes together by stressing that there is a tendency for those working with AIDS sufferers 'to over-use the positive and push away the negative—at some cost'.

The negative, however, was expressed in the shape of some scepticism about the role of psychoanalysis in the AIDS arena. AG said, 'One of the problems of homophobia is psychoanalysis'. This was supported by CF. AG's view was that analytic interpretations can be quite alienating. He saw them as philippic and punitive judgements, anti-love even. Earlier he had spoken of his vision of more cohesion in society, and now it became clear why he had been unable to explore it. He felt blocked and depressed. 'My peace of mind has been affected by AIDS'. I think this was a most valuable contribution and was maybe spoken from the darkest side of all of us.

Extracts

Profound sadness prevailed throughout the last plenary session, presumably as a result of good small group work, as well as the realization that a whole day's intense experience was about to finish. The following extracts are taken from the tape-recording. When the speaker's voice could be identified, the initials were used; otherwise points of ellipsis indicate that another contributor started speaking.

MP: We can now have an exchange of experiences, opinions, attitudes, questions, anything that you want to bring up now at the end of the day, and then there is a quarter of an hour from 4:30 to 4:45 to deal with possible future plans, but until then there is time for discussion. [3- to 4-minute silence.] What do people feel about the day? . . . Experiences? Inputs? Sharing? [Silence.]

AM: It is not easy to change from the experiential mode to the format of a plenary discussion.

JBa: The thing I am going to carry away from the day is the image that you—I am sorry I don't know your name—presented in the fishbowl, the image of infected people. I have been developing that over the last couple of hours. What really has left me quite surprised is why those who have got AIDS don't in fact get a blow-pipe and darts and go around darting us, the way that people with Kalesnikov rifles do, in Britain, who have been firing off at two or three innocent bystanders. That's what I'm left with. I don't know what it means, I don't know where it is taking me, I don't know what the implications are, but that's what I am going to take away from today.

. . . :   Our group was developing that theme. Having had a rather tough time in the morning, we were cohesive in the afternoon. We talked about AIDS as only one example of the pain inflicted on a wide range of unloved, agonized people by the complacent majority. The whitewashed majority don't want to know about it. They are trying to defend themselves. It makes me feel angry that AIDS influences them against the minority. They can't forget about it. But there are also a lot of angry feelings among the unloved people who have got this horrible condition that they want to attack the complacent, unloving people.

AM: In the fishbowl, on a deeper level, there was tremendous anger. It was against me. You beautifully expressed it with that image of the infected syringe which you attributed to others. And that is the sort of thing that often happens: the anger is very strong, it is directed towards the one who is actually responsible for the situation, but it cannot be expressed directly. Therefore, it gets diverted against someone else, against 'them'. You put it in a symbolic way.

AG: You are assuming that is the case. But what does one do with that information when one has got it? This is really my question about this sort of group analysis. I see, you know, the interpretation, the meaning of the unconscious forces, but what I am asking you is how does one use it for resolution?

AM: Well, you can only use it in the here-and-now. At this moment we are talking about something that has passed. What I said I said just to change the direction of this conversation, to get away from the experiential mode . . .

DE: Just going back to that. In the fishbowl it was used in a form of resolution. After Angela picked up the anger, various people in the group were much more in touch with themselves and their own feelings, and the group became more differentiated. I think that is very facilitating, and it does actually bring us back to the work with AIDS patients.

. . . :   What it put me in touch with was the regressive position into which people are pushed by AIDS. It reminded me of the very infantile wish that everybody be hurt . . . (very quiet) . . . out of a kind of narcissistic will . . .

. . . :   One of the things that has struck me today is the way we talk about working with AIDS, as if AIDS is an entity in itself, rather than the people. We keep on hearing it as if it stood on its own. Perhaps it does, in one sense. I don't know why but I find that quite difficult.

. . . :   I am surprised that a lot of people use the term 'AIDS victims' and 'AIDS sufferers'. You know, I think we really need reminding that it is very patronizing, maybe linked in with our fears. We need reminding that they are really ordinary people, that they are people with AIDS, not AIDS victims.

. . . :   But they are sufferers, surely?

CF: Can I pick that up too. I think you are right, and that is very important. But it sounds so trite when you just say it straight like that. The lady who spoke at the end of the fishbowl really put meaning into that when she said that 'Well, I know none who knows for sure he is not going to die tomorrow.' When I am sitting with an AIDS patient in my consulting rooms—perhaps one who has got KS—who may well survive five years, who is to know that I am not going to die of a stroke or a car accident in the next 12 months? And so we ought not to speak of people dying with AIDS. We should speak of people living with it. AIDS is, after all, a state of vulnerability. Most people with AIDS are not sick most of the time. They are vulnerable, but they are living until they get their next sickness. I think you are right that it is very important, and I say thank you to the lady who spoke at the end of the fishbowl.

. . . :   I wanted to say exactly the same as Charles: it is living with AIDS, not dying with AIDS.

JB: We speak of cancer victims and stroke victims. I think it is also important not to collude with the emotional denial that there is not a sense in which one is a victim of this terrible disease and is a sufferer.

. . . :   But would you like to be called a 'victim'? I know that patients get really angry when they are told 'you are a victim'.

JB: Well, I would not like to be a victim, but neither would I, I mean . . . I think that as much as being sensitive one also has to be aware of the reality. [Lots of voices.]

. . . :   It is like someone living with cancer then. Isn't it?

. . . :   Well, it is also like saying you are a victim and so you apportion blame to that person.

. . . :   We are all victims, all death victims, which is the other way around of looking at it. We are not all living; we are about to die.

CF: From the point of view of working with patients, though, we simply ought not to use this term. There are things that you learn when you work with these patients. There are things you do and things that you don't do. And one of the things you don't do is to use that word.

AM: It would be good if you could expand on why that is so.

CF: Well, I think it is the feeling of being controlled. If you are a victim, your death is inevitable. The patients don't want to see it that way. They want to see that they are living, and that they are going to live. And it is becoming more and more a reality now that we have various anti-viral treatments.

. . . :   People also die. And I think that has to be kept in mind.

CF: I don't think we are going to forget that.

. . . :   I am sure you are not, but I think there is a certain amount of denial sometimes with that situation.

. . . :   Yes, that is true, but then denial is not an inappropriate way for some people to function with illness.

. . . :   Well, we are all dying from the minute that we are born. We are all ageing and dying. But does that make us victims of life?

. . . :   To call someone a 'Person With AIDS' is just an attempt to neutralize words like 'victim'. It is as pure and simple as that.

. . . :   I think that people who have AIDS and, indeed, people with cancer feel very attacked by that. And that is where the victim bit comes in. They are experiencing an attack on the body and on the whole concept of themselves. They have been attacked by something that is alien to them and to their life and health. That is why people feel victims. It sets up all the persecutory anxieties and opens up a whole lot of early primitive stuff.

. . . :   I wonder about the life victims, those of us who are left behind. Given a few more years, every family in the country perhaps will have lost a member through this illness. Our small group was getting quite preoccupied with survival and guilt, also with loneliness and loss. That is another side that is very important, those who are left behind.

. . . :   Where the semantics continue to take us, I don't know. Perhaps the semantics are a defence against what I consider the most important part of the day. That was when the lady in the fishbowl—the fishbowl seemed to be a very powerful moment—when the lady said she felt that she was no longer reporting on her small group, but that she was under examination herself. In thinking about AIDS, thinking about what seems to be a sort of death notion brought so far forward, it has made us all look at ourselves. I was reminded of my own attempts of trying to approach various people within my hospital, to see what sort of work could be set up, and how I felt when my attempts were met by nervousness, territoriality and anxiety because a psychiatrist was approaching. . . . My approach actually forced people to look at themselves, while looking at their patients, looking at their own feelings. I thought that was very much part of the currency of the large and small groups today.

MP: That brings us to some sort of consideration about the value that people may attach to this particular way of dealing with the work. Quite a number of people said that they have been to many conferences—in fact, that there are too many conferences, and that choices have to be made. So it is a question of what kind of work this sort of meeting represents; is it significantly different, is it a help for those working with PWAs? I am slightly anticipating the last section of this discussion, but it is a question we have to address.

. . .:   In our group we were exploring the means by which we defend ourselves from the pain others experience. It was very useful to explore the feeling of hostility that some people have that this terrible illness exists which is going to affect us all. Then we got down to experiencing it on a more personal level and discovering the way in which we can actually relate to others' pain without resenting it.

. . .:   One of the constructive things for us to consider is how to help people who are troubled. They have a disease that they can pass on to others, but also because of knowing that, they experience hostility within themselves. The counsellor, the person who is directly responsible for the management of the individual patient, may be able to help a great deal in containing that hostility, which is in fact dangerous.

MP: Yes, indeed, the images we've used so far had to do with battle. Darts and blow-pipes and victims. But there are probably many people here who have not had any contact, I am assuming, with small group work in the same way as we experienced it today. I wonder if we could have some responses, observations, comments . . .

. . . :   My experience of working with small groups is different. I have always found the analytical approach very alien, and it's difficult to understand the point of it. But I am actually taking away a lot from today. I was forced to look at the group process and what happens in my own staff team, in our own community. Today went some way in changing my attitude towards group analysis.

AM: Perhaps we should ask for negative comments as well. The silence might cover up some dissatisfaction. . . . We could learn from it if you tell us what went wrong for you, what you expected that did not materialize, some disappointment that is likely to be there. . . .

. . . :   One of the things for me was more doom and gloom today about AIDS than I feel is realistic. We need to look at the hope, we need to look at the future and the hope for these people.

AM: I think you are pinpointing a polarity, because most people here are less closely relating to the dying patient than you are. . . . [Two people talking at the same time.] . . . The further away we are from the danger point, I think, the more gloomy we are. What struck me in St Stephens was the fantastic warmth and pleasant atmosphere, nearly exhilaration. . . . I felt it, too, every time I went there. I loved it. One becomes addicted to it.

MP: But there are people for whom the high point of their life has been, say, their wartime experiences, working with people in the face of danger and forming a very cohesive group.

AM: Absolutely, but there is a split there: over-using the positive and sort of pushing away the negative—at some cost later on in life or at the expense of other groups.

MP: This is a point, Antony, where I wondered if you might want to say more, because I think you spoke about the sense of possibly a false cohesion in society, that it was a brittle cohesion, that there was a sense of . . .

AG: I don't experience any cohesion in society at all at present. I think society is becoming more divided and antagonistic and hostile every day. People are splitting up into their own little embattled interest groups, which alienates practically everybody else. If I could go back to the earlier point though, Malcolm, I have heard an analytic interpretation that aroused intense hostility with a good many people, including me. It was said that people who have been despised and rejected by society all their lives can only attain a degree of love, attention and care by going to the extent of incurring their own death. That was what an analytically orientated observer felt in the war against AIDS in San Francisco. I found that very alienating. I, too, find analytic work somewhat difficult because whenever people come up with analytic interpretations, my understanding is blocked rather than helped. I feel I am having somebody else's perceptions imposed upon me. Thinking about that, I realize that when I am doing my own type of group work, I, too, am interpreting, perhaps in a different manner. I suppose one cannot do group work without interpreting in some way or another.

. . . :   Although I could say many positive things about today, what concerns me is this being called an AIDS workshop. I wonder whether that actually reinforces some of the stigma. What I am curious to know is whether those of us who actually don't work directly with HIV-positive people or with PWAs, whether those of us feel less fearful or more fearful after today . . . ? [Silence.]

MP: Well, can we have some response here? Less fearful, more fearful? Less pessimistic, more pessimistic? [Silence.]

AM: I just want to make a point to Jan. This workshop is called 'Group responses to the AIDS crisis.' It is about our responses. [Background noise.]

AG: I feel more pessimistic. What has been dawning on me is that this crisis is like a war. A battle has its own built-in excitement and a possibility of soon seeing the end of it. Whereas what has been dawning on me today is the chronicity of this whole thing. In a sense we are not into it yet, but I can see it really escalating right ahead in the future. I am perhaps one of the minority here who can remember the war and grew up in the war. The worst thing that AIDS has done to me is to take away the relative peace of mind I had hoped for in the last couple of decades of my life. Once again it is as if I am living in the early stages of the war, and I can see no prospect of peace coming. This is the phoney war, where we had all these leaflets, the Government seemed to think it would win the war by dropping leaflets on the Germans and on everybody else. People formed little groups to discuss what they would do, but they had never actually experienced an air raid or bombs dropping. Very soon a lot of those people are going to begin experiencing it, and there is not going to be an early end to it. My peace of mind and a lot of my potential happiness has been taken away from me. It is not just because I am a gay man, but what I see happening to the whole of society as the epidemic spreads.

. . . :   I am very concerned that until the bombs actually do drop on people, on the authorities, the money will not be there. People are not doing anything effective in terms of preventive health measures. The only way to get people to look positively at what they are doing to protect themselves from AIDS is through small group work. But, I don't know—is it all going to be too late?

. . . :   How do you get them into it? As I said upstairs in the small group, I was told at school that you can lead a horse to water but you can't make it drink. We have all these skills, but nobody seems to want to know about them, or not many people.

MP: When you spoke about getting people into small group work, just then, what were you meaning?

. . . :   The only work I see that has been useful with home helps and young people was providing at the very least a half-day when some factual information can be put in, but also role-playing sessions. It helps people to role play and feel what it is like to have a father who has got AIDS or a child who is infected. That is the only thing I have seen that has actually changed attitudes. The problem is that the authorities, those who have the money, are so frightened themselves. . . . The other thing that makes a difference is meeting and knowing somebody who has got AIDS. On the TV the other night there was a group of young people meeting in a cafe in Birmingham. They were discussing AIDS. Some came out with all the stereotypes and all the usual rubbish, all the avoidance, all the bad and unhelpful responses. As soon as a person with AIDS and another who was HIV positive were brought in, as soon as they met a real person, everything changed. It transformed what was going on in that group.

. . . :   There are several things I have been thinking and wanted to say. One is that compared with conferences, where there is a bombardment of information and one moves from one lecture to the next and you take notes and you are at the receiving end of it all, it felt very good to be part of something that was dynamic and involved. From that point of view experiential group work is very helpful. It also puts one in touch with other people from different disciplines whom maybe one passes by at conferences, but you don't actually get to have a conversation with.

. . . :   What has been useful has been the ability to begin to address, to deal with the feelings and the responses to the feelings rather than just the responses to AIDS.

MP: As you say, it is the beginning. So, the question is, what do we make of this beginning? Is there a wish for some sort of follow-through or continuation, accepting that the authorities are not going to provide money, that we are going to have to find our own resources for this? It is a question of what is feasible, what do people want, what the Institute of Group Analysis—with its own resources in terms of trained people—may be able to provide.

[Later:]

. . . :   I find it sad that the AIDS patients I have had in three different hospitals in the health service all said that the groups they were offered were disappointing. They consisted in discussing their symptoms as victims and exchanging factual information about where to get practical help. Because they were in a hospital, dependent on the hospital, they felt they had to be nice and smiling, otherwise they might not get treated well. They did not feel they could expose any negative feelings. I wonder about a patient group separate from a hospital . . .

. . . :   I will interrupt to say that there are many such patient groups. . . . Terrence Higgins Trust, London Lighthouse, Antibody Positive Group . . . As for hospitals, I can assure you that not all patients are hesitant to express negative feelings. Some of them are particularly articulate in that regard.

. . . :   But these groups are all what I call supported by the homosexual community. I just wondered whether a group even outside would have a beneficial influence.

. . . :   I think that the London Lighthouse might be very angry to hear you say they were solely supported by the homosexual community.

. . . :   The THT probably would be, too. They both see themselves as local organizations. In reality, of course, they do have many gay members.

. . . :   Well, certainly in the London Lighthouse there is a clear ideology that is very different from the psychoanalytic one here. People here may feel that the psychoanalytic one is rather concerned with death and gloom. I think that it is important that we have a range of approaches to be offered to PWAs.

. . . :   As I expressed earlier this morning, I thought that one of the problems of psychoanalysis is homophobia. Nevertheless, I think it is a pity that at the moment there is so little input from analytic approaches into treatment groups. People need different kinds of approaches. It would be nice to have something other than co-counselling.

. . . :   Precisely. That is why I came today.

[Later:]

. . . :   There is a lot of bafflement and frustration and anger among those of us involved in the AIDS field either as PWA or people working with PWAs, because of the pressure we are experiencing from groups out there. To experience that actually in group work would be good.

[Later:]

. . . :   I'd like to ask something slightly different. On one level I have got quite a lot from today, and I have got quite a lot from the speakers this morning. I don't want to knock the fact that we had the speakers. But for me, I came here expecting a group experience and want more of that. I go to a lot of conferences and hear a lot of speakers, and the group experience was too short. We were just beginning to touch on something, and it is the end of the day. I would ask for something a little longer and quite intense still. Also, I want an opportunity myself to explore some of the areas of sexuality. As a trainer, I spend time with other people, but I have nowhere to take that myself in a group.

[Later:]

. . . :   Can I go back to when we were talking about support for patients and staff. So many of the patients who become sick are in a financially embarrassed state, and they could not afford fees. I think that is a very important thing to bear in mind if we are going to offer support. . . . Somehow it has got to be funded.

MP: Well, this whole question of funding is something we shall have to start, and any information that anyone can give us about the channels to approach, we will use because a lot of you have got practical experience. . . .

Well, we have come really to the time for conclusion. So I want to thank you all very much for attending and on your behalf, through you, thank the convenors, Janet Boakes, Dorothy Edwards and particularly Angela Molnos and, of course, the speakers this morning for taking part.

CHAPTER ELEVEN

The participants' evaluation of the workshop

In the following participants' answers to the questions in the evaluation form (appendix VI) are given, subdivided into positive and negative reactions. Remarks and comments already quoted elsewhere are not repeated here. Most responses to the non-fishbowl and the small group experience appear in chapters 8 and 9.

Positive aspects of the workshop

'The workshop got off to a good start, with three excellent talks. CF brought the ill patient into the room, and his compassion and dedication to his work set a constructive mood, which continued throughout the day.'

'... It was refreshing that it was not a medically orientated workshop. ... A really stimulating and enjoyable day. Thank you!'

'The "best" part was everyone trying to understand and get in touch with real feelings. Lunch was very pleasant.'

'The whole workshop was a very positive experience for me. The "one day" was important in that I felt the urgency to get the work done. It did enable us to achieve a great deal in the time given—I have no idea how the workshop could be improved. It was well planned. The food was delicious. The accomodation ideal. Well done. Best wishes. Thank you.'

'CF was excellent for me. He has helped me a lot to see another side.'

'I was enlightened as to the depth of the emotional and psychological effects of the AIDS crisis on individual sufferers. As a result I also realize now the many implications for our society—other than seeking prevention and cure. For instance, who should decide the level of resource allocation? At what cost to other sufferers is the allocation of such resources?—The amount of knowledge acquired and emotional transition experienced in this workshop by a person like myself (who had felt already quite well versed on the subject . . .) gives me an idea of how ignorant and unaware the general public must be.—It has motivated me to continue learning and sharing my knowledge with others in an effort towards contributing to some relief of the AIDS crisis. . . . A day of exceptional quality. Thank you for an excellent workshop.'

'The sharing of the idea by AM of the "rational" me talking with the "frightened animal" me was very helpful. It allowed me to acknowledge my personal fear of AIDS to some extent, although this remains rather elusive! I found the opening remarks and all the speakers' contributions illuminating. It felt like a very rich experience.'

'Although announced as an "experiential workshop", the day began with talks by experts, useful for those of us who lacked direct experience of working with AIDS patients.'

'I had two or three conversations with other participants that were strengthening and reassuring—a feeling of being on the same wavelength.'

'It was useful to discuss the issues surrounding AIDS in a structured environment. It made a nice change to be able to talk about them in an intelligent and less emotive way. I have been to some seminars in which we (I include myself) all became very emotional and as a result were unable to examine the real issues.—Thank You!'

'All the speakers made interesting observations.'

'I very much more enjoyed the morning than the afternoon. MP and AM gave eloquent perspectives, whereas due to their frontline experiences, the presentations of CF and AG were much more "denial-laden". Altogether, a valuable beginning.'

'Meeting with other people and the small group experience.'

'Most positive aspect was the fishbowl. But the whole day was very useful and enlightening.'

'It surprised me to see how the absence of adequate support and role models leads to many carers getting damaged as well as limits their understanding of the multi-group dynamics in which their clients live and function. I also discovered some aspects of my own hypocrisy and my generation's lack of experience of a 'sex-death'–connection and fear. What will we reap from this in 20 years' time? The tight time boundaries worked well for me, especially around the input sessions. . . . I'm very glad I came. I would use your structure as the starting point for my own design for a day on AIDS at . . . Thanks.'

'Enjoyed and appreciated AM's contribution to the morning and felt uncomfortable during bits of CF's racy account of his work with AIDS patients. I think I was alarmed by the manic element. . . . A feeling that he was a skater and some of the ice was thin.'

'. . . reflective and constructive debate in the final plenary.'

'I found the opening session extremely interesting in lots of ways—mostly in the contrast between AM and CF. The presentation of AM had the direct simplicity that only wisdom brings. She seemed to be willing and able to observe and expose her own feelings and reactions with dispassionate honesty, for the purpose of improving knowledge. It's strange that I should use the word "dispassionate": it seemed to me a very important element in what AM was doing. A colleague of mine also at that workshop found her speech compelling because she was "so passionate". Yet, I don't think we were disagreeing. In great contrast to AM, CF was a wonderful example of energetic, self-sacrificing, fiery devil-take-it commitment with absolutely no reflectivity, no pausing to consider. He felt very noisy to me. This is not meant as disparagement in any sense. I greatly admire what he is doing and wholeheartedly support his crusading spirit. It is a time for firebrands. It's just that following AM, the difference was sharpened. And I was very moved by the respect with which the other speakers addressed him. I felt they were saluting his bravery and tacitly acknowledging his vulnerability without any hint of condescension.—After the small group experience, I don't worry so much about the staff group I am running. So, thank you for that! I enjoyed the day immensely. I had never been to the Institute before and was very pleased to find it a comfortable and friendly place. The atmosphere is pleasant and the staff helpful. Thank you for your care, concern and support.'

'Meeting other workers in the field was good. The speakers were interesting. . . . And the lunch was delicious!'

'I found the discussion on whether to call people with AIDS "victims" or not interesting, mainly because it made me think how easy it was to get into "prescribing", rather than asking what people want, as if there is one right approach we should all use. I think the workshop was very helpful.'

'I found all the speakers very good in their own ways. It was a great relief to find that the problems posed by AIDS on a personal and group level are now being looked at seriously to balance the mass of scientific and political communications.'

'Positive: Small group experience. CF's anecdotes at St Stephen's.The variety of backgrounds of the participants—beyond the usual IGA crowd!!'

'The fishbowl session was useful and positive.'

'The personal space that was afforded me by the sequence of small group / goldfishbowl exercise / small group, together with the material that was shared in the latter, allowed me to discover why my own response to the AIDS crisis has been somewhat flattened: I completed the hidden feeling / anxiety / defence triangle, which has been releasing for me. It was good being part of a group and not having to carry the responsibility for a course, to have informal personal contacts and to hear many differing responses. I got a lot from the day.'

'I enjoyed the introductory talks very much.'

'It was very refreshing to go on a study day where we left the facts and figures aside and thought about "feelings" and "responses".'

'How moving and appropriate the lectures and goldfishbowl were! The sense of everyone being involved. . . . Colleagues having similar feelings about their small groups.'

'I found the morning totally absorbing; I learned a lot and was stimulated to look at a lot of things differently. I thought the choice of speakers was excellent and particularly valued the variety of perspectives they offered.'

'The main inspiration and catalyst I think was the concentrated speech of AM in the morning—the view that irrational fear was the emotional basis in dealing with AIDS patients. I don't know if it is true, but surely it is inspiring! It was a good and warm experience to discover the open-mindedness of some of the participants. Especially the attitude of CF was encouraging. Some of the relief I got from the workshop was due to his attitude. A lot of different thoughts were stimulated by the workshop. . . . At the moment I am trying to write an article for a newspaper about the AIDS scene in my country. The workshop (plus the visit to some London hospitals) highlighted for me some of the dark sides of that scene: in my country the tendency to career-make and dog-fight seems to be the main feature at the moment.'

'The two male speakers gave the impression that the nature of the disease is so special that only homosexuals can really understand it and should be at the forefront in combatting it. I don't agree with this. Despite the sadness of the workshop's theme, I was pleased to come away with a few positive effects of the day: I received a lot of information, and I was reminded of the risks and the riches of everyday life.'

Negative aspects of the workshop

'Some participants who had done a lot of psychoanalysis kept on bringing up matters (e.g., death) in a calculated way, and I felt a trifle manipulated by this. We were seemingly tuned into totally different frequencies. I found some people's language difficult to understand.'

'Woolliness around confidentiality and boundaries. Re-sharing of group information was disturbing: I heard an information exchange on my way home on the tube regarding my own group members and others. Group analysis has a tremendous amount to offer, but colleagues who had never experienced this model were commenting and sharing their confusion over how safe it was! Thank you for arranging the day.'

'It was a pity that we, the "staff", withdrew to their own quarters during lunch and coffee breaks, as I would have welcomed more opportunity to talk informally with other participants.'

'Perhaps because of my particular "role" as general factotum, I felt rather "out" of the workshop. I was reminded of AM's vignette of the new team member who joins and cannot "join in" and only feels recognized when she is wanted to perform some menial task. It seemed an unusually hard staff team to join once the workshop started. Not so on our preliminary meeting. Tho' not unexpected, the criticisms of the use of language annoyed me and produced quite a primitive feeling of rage and helplessness. "Who do they think they are to legislate for language?" along with a helpless awareness of the utter futility of trying to change it and a sense of outrage and loss of personal integrity if I let it go. I felt "defiled" and a traitor. It was very strong.'

'The worst was to see how denial can result in a shallow level of engagement and caring. Raising issues in "long" sessions and leaving us wiser and sadder to wend our way home is the nature of the beast.'

'I sensed a very tense atmosphere, and I am not sure whether it was because we didn't meet as a large group, but some people went away "unsatisfied". One probably would get a "No, we can do it better" response from both within and on the fringe of the gay community. This territoriality became manifest at one point in the workshop.'

'Not so positive for me were the plenaries and lack of time for another small group.'

'Generally negative views of homosexuality held by the psychoanalytic establishment, which, along with the churches, has done so much to legitimize homophobia. On the catering side—the day was very expensive and the food/tea/coffee not very satisfactory. I'd set off at 5 a.m.!'

'The initial emphasis given by CF and AG on AIDS as a homosexual problem perhaps resulted in less later discussion of the problems of IV drug users and haemophiliacs who have contracted AIDS and of HIV-positive babies and their families.'

'There seemed to be much said about terminal disease and the feelings surrounding its sexual transmission, but I was surprised that very little was said about the position of the main affected groups—homosexuals and drug abusers—and their relationship to society as a whole and the group-ana-lytic / psychotherapeutic mainstream.'

'The afternoon was not nearly so good.'

'The negative experience for me centred around the start of the morning and the talks, which in another context I would have enjoyed immensely. I felt that this was an unfortunate concession to the usual conference format. I, and, I believe, others, came for group experiences and group exploration.'

'I became increasingly aware that I was angry about every-thing. It was not only the HIV infection and AIDS that I was angry about, but also my impotence and the feeling that even tho' I worked my butt off for my patients, ultimately there is nothing I can do to stop this deadly virus. I know that is something I have to work on with my therapist. The fishbowl and the emphasis on the doom and gloom. Thank you for allowing me to comment. . . . '

'Less positive: the time spent on the introductory and con-cluding plenaries, the latter having to come before ideas really had time to develop, which was a bit frustrating. I don't know how, on an introductory day, you could have done it differently though! You were obviously aiming at a very heterogeneous group.'

'I was disappointed in the plenary discussion. There was not enough time given for remarks and thoughts from the floor. . . . The small group representatives held the floor. Never-theless it was informative and a good way to wind it up.'

CHAPTER TWELVE

Lessons derived from the workshop

D espite a number of critical observations that can be made, it is no exaggeration to say that this was a very successful workshop. One of the nicest compliments we received was by a participant who wrote: 'I have no idea how the workshop could be improved.' Someone else wrote: 'It was difficult to know how much more we could have done in such a relatively short time.'

To a large extent, we achieved what we set out to do and managed to avoid the chaos to which many meetings on AIDS used to succumb (chapter 14), due to anxieties and emotions breaking through from the unconscious of the workshop as a whole. In fact, nothing went out of control. The exceptionally high over-60% return of the evaluation questionnaire is in itself a sign of the degree of good will and co-operation generated by the workshop. Participants themselves were puzzled by their own positive reaction: 'Why have I taken the time to answer this questionnaire when normally I don't?'

For anyone wishing to replicate a similar event with the aim of exploring group responses to HIV/AIDS, or any other subject that provokes intense anxiety, it is worth reviewing once more the pitfalls that should be avoided as well as the ingredients that were essential for success.

The long and patient planning and preparations certainly helped (chapter 5). We reached a wide range of participants with greatly varying experiences in the field of HIV/AIDS (chapter 6). We would have liked to interest more group analysts than we did. As increasing numbers of group analysts will work with HIV-positive people, their relatives and friends, this situation might improve in the future.

Leaders of self-help groups might have preconcieved ideas about the 'analytic establishment' and see group analysis as a competing method rather than a new avenue for co-operation. Lawyers and insurance people who battle with HIV/AIDS-related problems might fear to be attacked in a workshop where primary care workers are in the majority, the AIDS crisis is seen more from the point of view of the person affected by the virus, and there seems to be less sympathy for economic and legal considerations or even for the overall interest of society.

Why did we not have representatives of self-help groups, especially from the gay and black organizations? The fact is that our attempts to approach them did not lead to anyone from those groups wanting to participate in our workshop. The same applies to people working with haemophiliacs, the legal profession and insurance companies. We tried to include representatives of those groups as well but failed. A number of gay people were among the participants, but they did not represent any particular gay organization. The conclusion can only be that next time we need to try to find new ways of attracting their interest. Allowances will have to be made for presumably adverse assumptions and resistances such potential participants might harbour vis-à-vis group analysis.

As described elsewhere (chapter 6), the very positive, general atmosphere, conducive to self-reflection, was the result of a combination of factors—the type of participants present, including the staff, the careful preparations preceding the workshop, the genuine quality and great sincerity of the opening talks, as well as the friendly physical surroundings.

One problem to which it is difficult to find a good solution is what should staff be doing during the breaks. As it was, we quickly retreated into the staff room. The purpose was to exchange information among ourselves, check that everything was running smoothly, find out whether anything had to be rectified and give each other reassurance and support. Especially the small group conductors needed this space to relax and to have a brief exchange with colleagues before going back to their task. The undesirable side-effect of this arrangement was that we were isolated in the staff room and had no time to mingle among participants during the breaks.

When I myself stole out of the staff room to meet participants, I was further frustrated by discovering that from a normal talking distance I could not read the names on the participants' badges. They were typed in pale small print. . . . From correspondence and application forms, I knew each name and much more about everyone present, but I had no easy ways of putting a name to the person in front of me. The illegible badges irritated me greatly when I was conducting the non-fishbowl as well. In future workshops it would be advisable to write the names in large letters.

The four short talks (chapter 7), by MP (10 min), AM (20 min), CF (30 min) and AG (20 min), reflected the speakers' very different personalities. The variety of styles, especially the contrast between AM and CF, enhanced each other. The powerfully positive impact of these talks was due to various factors: the speakers kept strictly to their allotted time, they described experiences and observations in vivid, uniquely personal styles; facts and figures were left out altogether; theory was kept to a minimum; a series of shocking facts and controversial issues were highlighted. Only very few participants were disappointed by this opening because they expected experiential small groups and no talks at all.

There is no doubt that this was a good way to start. This kind of initial input serves to stimulate participants' thoughts and direct attention towards one's own and others' real experiences. What has to be avoided at all costs at the start of an experiential workshop is giving facts and figures about HIV/AIDS. Invariably these would be taken up by the groups as material for head-level discussions and as a defence against experiencing anxiety and emotions. If giving facts and figures is deemed necessary, this can be done after the experiential groups are over, at the end of the workshop. This latter format has been successfully tried out by the author in other one-day workshops.

Another effective device was the group / non-fishbowl / group sequence. Much has been said already about the non-fishbowl (chapter 8). This format needs to be managed with care and precision. The conductor of the central circle must be aware of all the possible pitfalls and able to contain exceptionally high degrees of anxiety. When asking the small group to appoint a representative to the non-fishbowl, the conductor might have to give a more exact idea than we did as to the unusual nature of the non-fishbowl. This anticipatory information to the groups has to be worked out exactly —neither too much nor too little—and agreed upon. The 'what, when and how' of what the conductor says about the non-fishbowl will have to be the same in all groups. We made the mistake of leaving this far too much to the individual conductor's discretion and last-minute decision.

We would like to take up the suggestion made by one of the participants that after the non-fishbowl, instead of having a break, everyone should go back immediately into their small groups to deal with the anxiety and the intense emotions.

The seven experiential small groups (chapter 9) were meant to form the core of the workshop. As it happened, they were slightly overshadowed by the success of the talks and the emotional impact of the non-fishbowl. What is essential is the careful selection of dedicated group conductors and well-prepared briefing sessions with them before the workshop (appendix III). In this we succeeded. Also, the meticulous work in composing the groups paid off. However, we were not quite ready to deal with the high number of last-minute drop-outs. Absences and hasty replacements distorted the structure (chapters 6 and 9). This eventuality has to be foreseen in future workshops. It is advisable to allow 15% to 20% oversubscription and compose groups correspondingly larger than the optimal size, thus allowing for a similar drop-out rate to the one we had. At the same time, late additions— when there is no longer time to think through the necessary re-structuring of the small groups—have to be resisted.

The last plenary session was a good meeting and a natural conclusion to a day's intense work (chapter 10).

Finally, the overall organization is worth replicating. The timing was extremely tight, and, thanks to a concerted team effort, it was adhered to exactly. The highly structured framework, the initial challenge by the speakers, the invitation to be self-reflective and the informal, friendly atmosphere created a safe holding environment in which to experience emotions and think.

Time and again intellectualization is mentioned as a defence against AIDS-related anxiety and distressing emotions. However, it must also be remembered that an experiential group or workshop is not meant to be a mere exercise in pouring out emotions. It is a learning experience in the course of which people do get in touch with their true feelings regarding the topic under discussion. They also gain a better understanding of what their emotions and anxieties mean in relation to themselves and the issue at hand. The constructive and congruent meeting of true feelings and intellect explains the remark made by a number of participants: 'I learnt a lot.'

CHAPTER THIRTEEN

Recommendations

I n the following we list the recommendations for future action that were made by participants and staff members in the last plenary session, in the group conductors' follow-up meeting of 27 February 1988, and in reply to question 3 on the evaluation form (appendix VI). An attempt is made here to put all the suggestions in distinct categories and place them in some logical order. The sequence does not necessarily reflect the importance or the feasibility of any particular suggestion.

1. Write up this workshop.

2. Repeat this workshop.
The most frequently suggested modification concerned its length: 2 days, a weekend, or even a week. Other suggestions were: to hold it in other parts of London, in the North, abroad; to address the existential, spiritual dimensions, fundamental questions about birth, love, death; not to have speakers, but to use the entire time for experiential groups; to start it with

a discussion on homosexuality; to add a large group session; to make more observations on the group process.

3. Establish ongoing support groups for the carers at GAS/IGA, elsewhere in London and the UK.

4. Establish an HIV/AIDS-related large group.

5. Start supervision groups for carers, counsellors of HIV/ARC/AIDS patients.

6. Organize short training courses in group analysis for carers, counsellors, group conductors who work with HIV/ARC/AIDS patients.

7. Explore similarities and differences between group analysis and other group approaches with those who are doing group work in the AIDS field.

8. GAS/IGA should act as a clearing house for information on group-analytic resources available for HIV/AIDS.

9. Use IGA-trained group analysts as consultants and group conductors in HIV/AIDS-related programmes.

10. Use GAS/IGA's existing programmes (e.g., January Workshop, Work Discussion Groups, Introductory Group Experience with co-conductors, GAS large group section).

Two suggestions, (9) and (10), made by staff members, were directed to the participants, inviting them to make use of existing facilities. How many participants might take up these ideas we do not know, but it is likely that such one-off invitations would not yield results. The following candid statement by a participant might speak for others as well. It shows that more active initiative on the part of the GAS/IGA is required if the two parties are to be brought into closer co-operation:

'I cannot say what else I would want from the Institute now, but that is not to say I didn't get anything out of the workshop. I hope that what I've already written makes it clear that I did. Perhaps you would be kind enough to let me know of any future plans that you have in this area of work. Although I don't know what I want, I may recognize it if I see it!'

Most of these recommendations place the burden of implementation on the GAS/IGA. Twenty months after the workshop only one, namely (1), is on the way to being implemented with the publication of this volume. Two others, that is (6), were initiated and then petered out. The reason is simply that the GAS/IGA, as other institutions, are already fully stretched with their existing programmes and have no free resources in terms of time, effort, physical space or finances to put into new initiatives. It needs considerable external pressure to add a new activity to an institution's existing programme. The heart-felt plea by participants for even a one-off workshop is not enough to move an institutional machinery. In conclusion, there seems to be an organizational impasse. The potential users expect the IGA/GAS to take the initiative, and the latter are resistant to engaging in additional work.

* * *

Here are some of the above-listed suggestions in the participants' own words:

'In the IGA you have a specialized area of expertise on offer and if you, in developing further training, can remember this, you will remain a useful source of "nourishment" for people like me who work in training. You would be a source also for people in the "AIDS establishment" who do not come on our courses because they consider they have the answers!'

'I found myself constantly wishing that I didn't have to travel so far in order to attend a workshop of exceptionally high quality. I live in the North of England and would suggest that any future activities of this nature be duplicated in

Manchester. I am confident that such workshops would be oversubscribed and therefore prove cost-effective. Thank you for an excellent workshop.'

'It would be most useful for IGA to explore various group approaches with others of us who use different techniques to analytic ones. AIDS raises such deep and far-reaching issues that we need to pool our collective insights.'

'The relationship between existential and common calamities of man and the situation of HIV-positive persons was mentioned in different groups, but it needs to be more elaborated as a theme—although it is very complicated. As an AIDS patient told me a week after London: "You have another diagnosis which leads to death: the name of the illness is life".'

'The workshop needs to be longer for issues of birth, death and love, for existential and spiritual aspects to be explored.'

PART THREE

Looking towards the future

CHAPTER FOURTEEN

Strange phenomena

T hroughout Part 2 there are hints at some unexpected, apparently inexplicable and strange turns of events. If we really tried, we could explain each in itself, dismissing it as one of the many difficulties encountered in the process of organizing any workshop, regardless of its theme. However, looking at all these occurrences together, the more plausible hypothesis is that unconscious collective anxieties around HIV/AIDS might have contributed to the accumulation of strange phenomena. Some were threatening the workshop's success from the most unlikely side, from those who wanted it to succeed—friends, colleagues and the organizers, including myself. The strange phenomena are a threat from within, eluding our awareness at the time, like the retrovirus dormant in the immune system.

Discouragement by friends, and the initial enthusiasms of others who were ready to co-operate in the Workshop and then changed their minds, marked the early stages. Also, my own sudden experience of panic (chapter 4) can be counted among the first strange phenomena. In the preparatory phase, there was the curious lack of response on the part of group analysts other than those who formed the workshop's staff. Also, I noticed a number of bungled actions and minor misunderstandings between highly co-operative colleagues. My attempts to involve other institutions were met by unusual silences and, more amusingly, on a few occasions were followed by invitations a little later to attend other workshops organized by them. The Freudian slip of using the word 'experimental' when referring to our 'experiential workshop' in some correspondence said a lot about unspoken doubts. However, it seemed extraordinary that the same slip should occur in a circular letter typed in our own office! After all, an experiment can go wrong.

Some events immediately before and during the workshop were puzzling, above all the unusually high rate of last-minute drop-outs. There were participants who had paid, wanted to come and could not because of sudden illnesses, a bereavement, other problems in the family, and so on. My own illness had a physiological basis, but in retrospect it is clear that repressed anxiety was a contributing factor in the depths of my own unconscious where psyche and body meet.

During the workshop the major mishap was that, contrary to our plans, the talks were not recorded—a collective 'over-sight' on the part of us, the organizers. We all failed to notice until it was too late that the tape-recorder had been wrongly connected up. . . .

There was another bizarre occurrence around tape-recording. About four months after the workshop, a colleague of mine reminded me that we had decided not to tape-record the non-fishbowl session. It was a shock and a double realization: first, my unconscious had chosen to forget our original decision; second, in the absence of a verbatim record, I now had to piece it together from a variety of uneven notes, recover it from the recesses of an unreliable memory. And yet I had been aware all along of how memories fade and memories of emotions in particular get distorted.

* * *

There was a time when my dentist did not wear
rubber gloves. . . .

AM

In the outside world, observing the changes taking place in
daily life and scanning the weekly news for every scrap of
information between the end of 1986 and early 1989, I identified a lot of confusion and strange phenomena around the
AIDS epidemic. It seemed to me that all press reports about
HIV/AIDS, from the nonsensical to the meaningful, their
form of presentation and contents, could be grouped into the
following categories:

1.   objective facts [mostly giving cause for justified concern];
2.   unavoidable havoc [as a direct consequence of (1)];
3.   prejudice [resulting mainly from unconscious group
     responses to (1) and (2)];
4.   confusion [which could be avoided if (2) and (3) were to be
     understood and accepted]; and, finally,
5.   language distortions, symptomatic of (3) and (4).

What has been said so far in this book throws some light on
each of these aspects of the AIDS crisis. Here I would like to
give a few examples of (4), i.e., the confusion and the strange
phenomena that go with it.

* * *

One of the most extraordinary public confusions appeared
in newspapers, radio and TV in April 1988. By all accounts, it
stemmed from within the very hospital that had to endure its
consequences. It was reported that a Devonshire doctor, who
was born in Zimbabwe and had practised there as a surgeon
for five years, had died of AIDS. The following, absurdly
contradictory messages and explanations appeared in quick

succession on subsequent days: (a) all 340 patients on whom this doctor had operated should come forward for counselling and possible blood tests; (b) no one should worry because there is no danger whatsoever of a doctor transmitting the virus to a patient; there is no one single known case . . . ; (c) the doctor was unaware of being infected; (d) he had contracted the virus while operating on AIDS victims in Zimbabwe. . . . One would like to ask some questions such as: Why (a) if (b) is true? How come that a patient can infect the surgeon (d), but a surgeon cannot infect a patient (b)? If (c) is true, from where does the information (d) come? and so on. The hospital received hundreds of telephone calls, but very few were by that doctor's patients.

Strange phenomena and confusion used to appear in workshops and conferences on AIDS. In a study-day on children and AIDS at a prestigious hospital attended by a couple of hundred knowledgeable AIDS workers in February 1988, very little was said specifically about children. There was much boredom in listening to well-known general facts and figures about AIDS, until a middle-aged policeman appeared on the platform. With the aid of an old video about junkies, he tried to lecture the audience about the disgusting habits of drug addicts. There was a mini-revolution, and he was shouted down so that he could not finish his talk.

There are numerous other examples of an AIDS workshop ending up in a shambles or being taken over by a vociferous minority and its structure being destroyed. In early summer 1987, the Third International AIDS Conference with 6,000 delegates was held in Washington. A well-known French researcher 'caused confusion when he fled from the conference hall after his talk and turned away all questions on his early findings (on an experimental vaccine)'. There were boos and hisses when the official proposals to screen immigrants and prisoners and to start routine testing in hospitals and clinics were presented. The atmosphere was more like a football match than a learned gathering (*Sunday Times*, 7 June 1987).

By contrast, the Fourth International AIDS Conference with 7,500 delegates from 130 countries held in Stockholm a year later (12 to 16 June 1988) was perfectly organized and smoothly run and remained undisturbed. There were three thousand poster presentations, nine parallel sessions of papers, a symposium on the humanitarian side of AIDS, several satellite meetings, a commercial exhibition, and a simultaneous computer conference. 'To many of the guests . . . the prospect of this Swedish banquet, . . . was not particularly appetising, . . . In the event, the ingredients were so skilfully blended, the portions so finely judged, the courses so meticulously planned, and the service so unobtrusively attentive that head chef Prof. Lars Olof Kallings and his team earned the compliments of even the most fastidious diner' (Steel, 1988, p. 54).

Whether for better or worse, things seem to be changing. At the moment (1989), the AIDS issue is less at the centre of public awareness than it was a year or two ago. As a result, many seem to have forgotten the cautionary warnings about risk-taking with unsafe sex. On the other hand, the confusion around it seems to be on the point of clearing. Perhaps we are getting collectively used to living with this retrovirus. There are physiological parallels to this learning to live with the immune virus. Researchers found that 30% to 70% of African green monkeys are SIV-infected, yet they show no sign of immunosuppression or of SAIDS, and there is no long-term adverse selection pressure on the species (Essex & Kanki, 1988, p. 48). It is dangerously tempting to hope that mankind, too, might become HIV-resistant, physically and psychologically.

It might be that sometime in the future medical science will find a way around the retrovirus called HIV. But will the strange phenomena accompanying the outbreak of the AIDS pandemic disappear altogether or continue under other disguises? Was it a coincidence that the collective salmonella-in-eggs hysteria broke out 48 hours after the day designated to be World AIDS Day in December 1988? Why precisely then? Nothing dramatic had happened except in the public's mind. The danger of food poisoning through salmonella had been known for years. Why did World AIDS Day or the connection between the two go virtually unnoticed? Displacement of unacceptable or unbearable anxieties and emotions from one object to another is a mechanism described by depth-psychology and with which psychoanalysts and psychotherapists are familiar. It operates in both, the individual and the collective unconscious. By definition, such unconscious processes by-pass our collective awareness. We all participate in them. No one seemed to notice the displacement of anxiety from one health hazard to another. Of course, it is easier to dispose of hundreds of thousands of allegedly infected eggs than of the HIV infection that is inexorably advancing in our midst. Two months later, in February 1989, the collective anxiety concerning the threat to our health had reached an obsessional peak in this country. Apparently to the exclusion of all other news, the media gave prominence to reports on salmonella, listeria, Legionnaires' disease, Alzheimer's disease, water contamination, bovine spongiform encephalopathy, scrapie, and Cornish butter laced with mercury, urgently withdrawn from supermarkets. Obsolete health hazards, such as lamb's meat contaminated by the Chernobyl nuclear fallout, were revived. The headline 'The World Is Dying' appeared in very large letters, referring to environmental pollution. Meanwhile HIV and AIDS had disappeared from public awareness. Looked at more closely, all the above are interrelated and related to the AIDS pandemic in a variety of ways. The links remain unnoticed to protect us against the real anxiety that our very existence is under threat. Just to mention one unnoticed connection—both BSE in cattle and AIDS in humans cause dementia, are so far incurable and seem to be shrouded in some dark mystery. At the same time, compelling headlines also brought the evil and the sinister into focus, such as the 'cannibalistic' feeding of battery hens, cannibalism in Japanese prisoner-of-war camps, sale of human kidneys for transplants and so on. Together with AIDS, all related to the threat to our existence in the collective unconscious.

CHAPTER FIFTEEN

Group-analytic
and other group work
in a world that lives with AIDS

I n this last chapter, I would like to argue for a variety of
group approaches and at the same time indicate the
multiple ways in which group analysis may fulfil a significant role by offering the necessary theoretical background as well as the constructive spirit of co-operation,
tolerance and reciprocal acceptance. There is also a need for
substantial group-analytic contribution where boundaries
are concerned and specific skills are called for to recognize
and deal with unconscious undercurrents in groups. On the
other hand, we group analysts have to learn a great deal
about the new threats HIV/AIDS poses to the functioning of
groups.

We are all involved

Patients in therapy groups bring the AIDS crisis to the group analyst. Whether she likes it or not, she can no longer ignore it. Group members talk about their anxiety of contracting HIV infection or perhaps already having contracted it. Whether or not they are changing their sexual habits might be discussed. Someone remembers a short period of promiscuity in his past, a one-night stand or a drug-addicted partner five years back. They question, advise and support each other in their fear of AIDS. They wonder whether or not they should have the test and what good it does to know. Then, one day, a group member discloses that he is HIV positive. The conductor finds herself in a totally new situation, with an anxiety-ridden group seized by primitive fear and rage about having to tolerate the alien virus in their midst. Suddenly, strange phenomena occur in the group. Things seem to get out of hand for no apparent reason. The group conductor begins to feel that she cannot cope any longer.

The ultimate challenge to the group and its conductor will come when the HIV-infected member starts to develop visible symptoms, misses sessions and finally dies. Will the group as a whole be able to rise above the psychotic impulses unleashed in the depths of its shared unconscious? Will it be able to remain honest and open, to hold together, to hold him up to the end and to do it with genuine concern, care and warmth? Or will the group destruct itself as the only way out, its only avenue to run away from death? By disintegrating, the group abandons the member who has no escape routes. He is the only one who cannot flee death. For him, the group might be the only place where he could be himself and be entirely free to talk. Its disintegration might mean his being left to utter loneliness in his hour of greatest need. . . . This scenario is bound to happen with increasing frequency unless group analysts prepare themselves by studying the emotional concomitants of HIV/ARC/AIDS and by anticipating the most likely group responses.

Group versus secrecy and isolation

The sudden feeling of isolation and alienation from one's nearest and dearest is perhaps the worst aspect of being told that one has HIV. Whether or not there is a real threat of being attacked, ostracized or abandoned by family, friends, workmates or acquaintances, subjectively the situation could hardly be worse. The remedy of choice should be a group—any group the person can learn to trust and which deserves his trust. A well-functioning group is the best basis for support in such a personal crisis.

One of the reasons has to do with secrecy. Although a few people sometimes talk about their HIV infection without inhibition, more frequently the person who has learned he is HIV positive feels unable to tell anyone. The unspoken, dreadful, often guilt-laden secret assumes enormous proportions, and the rightly or wrongly anticipated isolation becomes a self-fulfilling prophecy. If the HIV-infected person can join a peer group with people who are in the same predicament, even if it is a short-term group set up ad hoc or an ongoing therapy group, he can be helped to use it as a testing ground to try to be more open about his physical condition and his emotions. The group can discuss the topic itself: the pros and cons of disclosing the truth about one's health status, how and when to share it with whom, with whom not to share it, and how difficult it is to cope with the reactions one gets. Others who have already gone through the experience might tell the group all about it and give useful advice.

Discussing specific topics and advice-giving occurs in all groups. Although it is not part of the group-analytic technique to encourage it, group analysts will recognize how invaluable such a discussion and advice-giving can be in this context: through it group members give each other strength to break the wall of silence that isolates them from the rest of the world. They teach each other, directly and by their example, inside and outside the group, to overcome fear and start communicating. The goal is an eminently group-analytic one: to learn to verbalize and communicate whatever is hidden and blocking one's functioning and is in the way of important relationships.

As HIV infection spreads, and the general public come to feel more and more threatened, the isolation of HIV-positive people and those who have AIDS is bound to increase. In a situation of mounting epidemic, the value and importance of peer groups for information exchange, mutual support and advice cannot be overestimated. Members draw strength from each other in adversity. The group is important to them: 'I don't have any other contact. I appreciate the togetherness.' 'We find it useful to talk, whatever else we do.' (Christ, Beckham, Galo-Silver & Shipton Levy, 1988).

Some might argue in favour of individual counselling on the grounds that every case is unique and therefore has to be dealt with individually. The premise is true—yes, every case is unique—but the conclusion is false. Group analysis has taught us that the individual's uniqueness and particular psychological needs are best taken care of in a well-functioning group. The one-to-one counselling can be an introduction, in some cases an important or even essential preliminary stage before joining a group.

Groups for the carers:
sharing the uncertainties

The involvement with HIV pre- and post-test counselling and with ARC/AIDS patients makes primary care workers more unsure about what they are doing than with any other type of patients. The uncertainty is both emotional and professional. The answer can only be in organizing ongoing staff support and supervision groups. Ideally, every worker should be in such a group.

Unlike psychotherapists or group analysts, on the whole primary health care workers have traditionally not been trained to deal with massive anxiety and overwhelming waves of emotions coming from patients and surfacing within themselves. Often they have even been misdirected in this respect, and the stoical front is viewed as professionalism and strength: 'You just put up with it, dear, and carry on doing what you have to do!' Most of those trainers and their pupils don't realize that though emotions can be suppressed, they do not go away but reappear in disguised and insidious forms, such as as displaced, inappropriate anger against colleagues (chapter 4) or some strange phenomena (chapter 14). The latter are mostly destructive or self-destructive acts and by and large unpredictable. In the first place, staff support groups have to help their members get in touch with their true feelings, including their anger with each other and with their patients.

The emotional stress for the carer seems to be worse than around other terminal illnesses. The main sources of this HIV/AIDS-related stress have already been described: the reactions of society at large to the AIDS epidemic, the emotional reactions of the individual patients and some of the group responses in institutional settings. The primary health care worker is exposed to all this at once. Specifically, he has to contend with the emotional bombardment coming from the unconscious of highly strung, anxious people, one after the other, the whole day long. They may be people who decided to have the test or patients already on the ward. In addition, there might be an 'atmosphere' at the working place due to the cumulative effect of everyone's anxieties, unsatisfactory working conditions and the management's failure to tackle effectively many problems at once. On the AIDS ward, the stress escalates further because of having to cope with the sometimes gruesome deaths of mostly young people with whom the staff had formed close relationships. Not one, but three, four or more deaths a week, and no time for mourning. Even when someone attempts to talk about the deaths in a staff meeting, it becomes a list of names, one of the items on a long agenda. . . . There is no place to express one's pain, sorrow and helplessness.

Professional uncertainty surrounds HIV/AIDS for the primary care worker, especially the physician. The age-old values and attitudes on which the relationship between the patient and the doctor are based have been put in disarray. The doctor is no longer the authority who knows best about what is good for the patient. The latter might know as much, or more, about his condition and the treatment possibilities as most of those who try to take care of him, including not only his GP, but also his highly trained specialist. Motivated by the hope of spotting news about a scientific break-through or a miracle cure from an unexpected quarter, the average educated patient might start reading every bit of information he can get hold of. In the process he becomes an HIV/AIDS expert and might greet his overworked doctor with a question about the latest report on such and such a drug trial in a particular scientific journal. While the patient has time to read and think, the doctor has not. Like other primary care personnel, he is too busy pushing himself through the professional pain barrier from one unresolved crisis to the next. The rapidly evolving technology around HIV/AIDS, combined with the lack of time to keep abreast of scientific progress, can undermine professional self-confidence.

An AIDS patient might refuse the treatment prescribed because it is too frightening or painful or simply because he has decided to die. Often the doctors themselves offer an AIDS patient the choice between various courses of action or inaction. At times it is the AIDS patient who suggests his own treatment. However, an overstressed doctor might panic and order the treatment to save the patient's life against his will. Such an act causes horror and deep distress, not only in the patient, but also in others caring for him. The treatment of AIDS patients, and when to discontinue it, the handling of information about them, are just some of the ethical dilemmas that add to the doctor's growing doubts and insecurity.

The relationship between the patient and his doctor can become peculiarly complex. The medical specialist's uncertainty about the length of time any patient with AIDS can be saved from one life-threatening crisis to the next brings with it a certain loss of medical power and authority. This, however, is often replaced by greater openness, warmth and compassion, one of the truly positive by-products of this epidemic. The patient is struggling with a dreadful and lethal condition, and the carer is overstressed. Others, those who have nothing to do with HIV or AIDS, appear to ignore or reject them both. Thus, the temptation to take refuge in each other's affection is great. Either of them can suffer deep emotional hurt if expectations of exclusive devotion are not met. Both the patient and his carer can do without additional hurt.

Not knowing where and how to set the boundaries of one's conduct with the patient on the continuum between cold clinical aloofness and intimate personal friendship is another source of professional insecurity. Frequently, confusion surrounds the setting of time boundaries as well. For instance, when counselling distressed people before and after their HIV test, workers are often reluctant to keep to time-limits. If the counsellor is not trained in the psychodynamic need for setting boundaries, he will feel guilty, whatever he chooses to do—guilty either towards the demanding patient for not giving him more time, or towards all the others who are waiting while he attends to the former. Such persistent guilt feelings may aggravate professional insecurity.

There is an overwhelming case for establishing staff support groups at all levels, a need that is widely recognized by most who work in the field. However, as has been hinted at earlier, this is by no means an easy task. There are enormous unconscious resistances against such groups being formed and considerable difficulties in holding them together once they have started. The group-analytic understanding of these resistances and difficulties is essential if we are to overcome them.

Support group for health advisers
at the Praed Street Clinic

by Kate Partridge

The following is a slightly adapted version of a report written
by Kate Partridge, Health Adviser at the Praed Street Clinic,
St Mary's Hospital, West London. It refers to a weekly 90-min-
ute session I have been conducting with the health advisers'
team since July 1987, of which she is a member. The need to
write this account, which has the approval of her colleagues
and their manager, arose spontaneously within the group. I
gladly offered to include it here. The other members of the
team were Jenny Davis, Vincent Moss, Liz Rose, Lyn Thom-
son and Pam Wilson.

Praed Street Clinic is one of the largest STD clinics in
Europe. At first the job of the health advisers—formerly
called contact tracers—consisted in seeing all clients with
gonorrhea and syphilis in order to offer them health education and pursue their contacts. As the HIV-1 infection and
AIDS appeared and started to become more common in
London in 1984–1985, the health advisers' work changed
dramatically.

We began to counsel all clients who wanted to be tested for
possible HIV infection, both before the HIV-1 antibody test
and afterwards, and we gave them their results. The
nature of our job had changed; instead of dealing with
infections that could be treated and cured, now we were
advising people about an infection that was potentially fatal.
The worries and fears this threat brought up in the clients
were enormous and varied. It also meant that we were seeing
a greater number who presented us with a wide range of
anxieties. As an STD clinic covered by the VD Act, ours was
one of the few places where confidential testing could be
guaranteed. We attended not only to clients with fears of the
HIV-1 infection due to sexual transmission, but also trans-

mission via intravenous drug use through the sharing of needles.

During the period from September 1986 to August 1987, and especially during the government's AIDS publicity campaign, the numbers coming to the clinic for HIV-1-related problems were vastly increased. It was during this period that three of the four health advisers developed stress-related symptoms affecting their physical well-being. They needed sick leave of between two and four weeks and even on returning were not able to take on their full share of the work load. The result was added pressure on the other members of the team, which led to further stress-related problems.

Our manager, Dr Deirdre Cunningham, then suggested that some form of staff support group was needed; we, the health advisers, agreed, and, Angela Molnos was brought in from outside the Health Authority to set it up. Originally we assumed that a forthnightly group of one hour's duration was all that was required. However, Angela was adamant that it would not be sufficient and insisted that far more was needed. Finally, a regular group session was agreed on a six-month trial basis, to be held between 10:00 and 11:30 each Thursday morning. During this time no health adviser would be available in the clinic. Clients who normally come to the clinic without a previous appointment could arrange to return later that day.

When the support group was first set up, there were a number of difficulties within the group itself as well as coming from other personnel in the clinic.

At first, the health advisers found it hard to accept the above arrangement: it seemed unimaginable that the Clinic could be left without cover in the middle of a working day and that no major crisis would occur during those 90 minutes. Guilt at not being 'where the clients were' was great. It took us some time before we realized that we would be able to give better care to clients if we started to look after ourselves and attend to our own needs in the first place. The group members also had to learn to trust each other well enough to discuss the many problems—not only practical, but also emotional—that were inherent in health advising. The fact that we as a team had been giving informal support to each other and were already a closely knit group made it easier to reach this level of trust, although it did not happen immediately.

There were also difficulties between the health advisers and other staff members in the clinic. A support group is very unusual within the NHS, and it was not surprising that there was some resistance, not so much to the idea, but to its actual implementation. There were two major areas of discord. First, exception was taken to the health advisers not providing a continuous service. Secondly, there was some feeling of 'Why the health advisers?' In time the problems were resolved. Gradually the clinic staff realized that the smooth running of the service was not adversely affected and that clients were always seen, even if it was not on that morning. The second question was more difficult to answer. The health advisers decided to suggest that if other personnel wanted a support group too, then they should ask for one to be set up.

During the 18 months that our support group has been functioning, it has proved its worth in many ways. There has been a major decrease in stress-related physical symptoms. The problem does not go away for good. However, we have learnt the importance of 'looking after yourself', which can and has been achieved in different ways. The one that is used by all the team is the support group. Other ways have been opting for part-time work, getting individual counselling and learning relaxation techniques such as massage. Though all these are important, what is essential for the team is to talk over the problems together. Moreover, the team was increased from 4 to 5 members.

The support group has allowed us regularly to discuss individual problems as well as questions concerning the practical running of the team. It has enabled us to know each other better and trust each other more. This must help provide a better service in a field where communication is such an essential part of the job. On discussing the support group, all health advisers agreed that it is essential to have

it. On the other hand, everyone pointed out that it is not an
easy option and that it takes hard work to make it a success.
Most of the group said that they found it very hard to talk
freely when they started and that some time elapsed before
the benefits became obvious.

Support groups are still very rare within the NHS. However, it is important that in high-stress areas, such as work
in the AIDS and HIV-1 field, more ongoing groups should be
set up. There is a very fast turnover of staff in these areas,
and if more effort to overcome the 'burn-out' problem is
required, then the support group is one underused tool.

I would like to thank my colleagues, the health advisers at
the Praed Street Clinic, for their comments on this report, Dr
Deirdre Cunningham for her support and our group conductor, Angela Molnos.

26 January 1989

The use of non–group-analytic techniques

A wide range of non-analytic techniques are being used
successfully in groups with health care personnel, with HIV-
positive people and with ARC/AIDS patients at various
points in the health spectrum from symptom-free status to
the last stages approaching death. The following examples
and illustrations originate mostly from a special session on
'The role of group therapists in the AIDS epidemic' at the
Forty-fifth Annual Conference of the American Group Psychotherapy Association, held in New York, February
8–12, 1988 (Christ et al., 1988; Wagner, Fuller & Nelson,
1988).

In that session the audience was asked by one of the speakers: 'Have you ever shaken hands with someone who has
AIDS?' Then those present were requested to put their right
hands on the table, close their eyes, imagine that handshake

and get in touch with their feelings. Such guided imagery can help to make people quickly aware of what they actually experience.

Role play can be a great help too. In a group of primary care workers an emotionally most instructive psychodrama was enacted. The following roles were assigned: lover, the dying AIDS patient, priest, mother, father, doctor, nurse. Everyone played a role he does not have in real life. Although there was no script, the improvised drama followed on from what the group had already discussed. They had talked about how each professional would feel in front of the dying patient and what problems each of them would have. Now they were exploring the emotions in others too. The role-play drama intensified, right up to the bitter end, when the father spoke: 'I feel I've lost everything, not only my son (who is gay, has AIDS and is dying), but also my wife (who has always defended the son). All my life I wanted to be strong. I feel I am not strong if I give in to this (i.e., forgiving his son, as everyone present asked him to do). I cannot do it.' Soon after that, someone said, 'It is over. He is dead.' No one, neither actors nor audience, could remain unmoved by the intensity of the play.

Another example of non–group-analytic technique is a time-limited group of six once-weekly sessions only. The group is composed of people who had come to a centre to donate blood, but whose HIV test showed that they were positive. They had no pre-test counselling. Most are well, but naturally very worried. The goal is to help them overcome the initial shock, organize further support and change their behaviour so that they don't infect others. Each session lasts 90 minutes, but as peer contact is considered the best help, members are encouraged to come half an hour earlier to the centre and have a cup of coffee (several come directly from work) and to socialize with each other also on other occasions outside the group. The six sessions are psycho-didactic in character and highly structured around the following topics: contract, learning health status self-assessment; issues of daily living; health and stress management, progressive muscular relaxation, use of imagery; communication (i.e., whom to tell or not to tell); safer sex practices; future options and organizing steady peer support.

Yet another group is composed of gay men who have KS and have been diagnosed as having AIDS. Their average survival time is about five years. Some patients say that, because of the disfigurements KS produces, they would prefer to have PCP (with less life expectancy). This is an open, on-going group that has been in existence since 1982, one hour a week, co-led by two social workers. Speakers are invited. Topics are chosen by the group: nutrition, stress reduction, treatment options, legal issues, safer sex and so on. When there is no speaker, then it functions more as a support group. Every possible subject relevant to their situation is discussed, among others the perceptions they have of their looks. The body image is important, as the disfigurements caused by KS can be devastating. They advise each other—e.g., 'Cover up the lesions with make-up, use shirts with long sleeves and go back to the gym!' The conductors try to teach tolerance all round—for instance, towards members who prefer different treatments—and to encourage them to have a good rapport with their physician. The group also helps members with suggestions for techniques to manage the side-effects of treatments and so on. When they really know each other, they start talking about emotions and then, later on, even about death. Suicide is sometimes discussed as an option. Although it rarely happens, talking about it seems to help. It gives them the feeling that they have some control.

A last example is that of a group of AIDS patients, volunteers in a medical research project. They used to come to the clinic, and they talked to each other while waiting. Someone on the team had the creative idea of making the most of their spontaneous contact with each other and form a regular group. Members of the group are at roughly the same stage of illness, and all receive exactly the same treatment and are subject to the same kind of demands. Some physicians involved in the research are also group members. The group gives continued strong emotional support. Patients discover in their midst different reactions to the same situation: 'To come to this hospital reminds me that I am ill', says someone, while another member points out: 'To come here makes me feel safe.' The physicians share their feelings about what they are doing. They learn more about their patients and learn from them. The group talks about gradual death, having to give up more and more (job, work, shopping, house chores, etc.), the constant adjusting to loss of functioning and the need to build up more support. 'Rational suicide' and the decreasing quality of their lives are explored. They hold on because of people who care for them. Yet someone requests: 'Put me to sleep when I reach that point. I don't want the respirator.' Then the doubt: 'Will the doctor honour a living will?' The motivation of these patients to participate in the demanding research project is their need to leave something behind—a sacrificial legacy for others.

The group-analytic thread

Group analysis offers the theoretical background to lend strength to all sorts of group initiatives in the AIDS crisis. In its founder's words, one of the applications of group analysis is 'to treat particular groups with regard to their specific group problems' (Foulkes, 1964, p. 52). Group analysis gives us the means to study 'what is the configuration of situations of tension and stress in the group; what conditions in the group and the individuals—two aspects always interrelated—precipitate crises in the particular way in which they do. That and why, for instance, a disturbance focuses on a particular individual' (ibid., p. 99). It also helps us to understand inter-group tensions better and why a disturbance focuses on a particular group and not on another. These questions are crucial in the institutional difficulties that surround the AIDS epidemic.

What I mean by 'group-analytic thread' is both: on the one hand, the possibility to look at any group in the light of group analysis, on the other the adaptation of the group-analytic method to ever new situations. Group-analytic principles can be usefully applied to a variety of groups, conducted along different lines, which, as we have seen, are needed, depending on the particular situation and on the short- and long-term goals to be achieved. While we can look with a group-analytic eye at all sorts of groups and group processes, an adaptation of our techniques to the total situation will always be required. Even if it is deemed useful to establish an analytic group for staff or patients, its boundaries will have to be re-set and its rules adjusted to the situation and its members' particular needs. In this way, with its double emphasis—on considering the total situation first, and then taking into account all aspects of it in painstaking detail—group analysis gives us practical guidance as well.

Let us take the case of a staff support group whose members work closely together as a team all day long, five days a week. Some of them even socialize with each other outside working hours. The group analyst sees them once a week for 90 minutes in the group session only. These simple facts constitute a total situation that is just the opposite to that in a group-analytic therapy group. In the latter members don't meet outside the group at all, they don't even know each others' family names or places of work or addresses, while the group conductor does. The group-analytic approach consists in both cases of taking care of the group as a whole in order to help the individuals in it. To achieve this same goal, the initial task of the conductor in both groups will be different: in the staff support group, where members are far better acquainted with each other than with her, the outsider, she has to make herself and her role accepted and prevent the group from isolating her. In the case of the therapy group, one of the conductor's main tasks is to wean the group early on from being centred on her person and from excessive dependence on her. In both cases she will use group-analytic techniques, mainly continual monitoring of unconscious and conscious communications and, if the group itself fails to do so, translating the unconscious tendencies into conscious verbal communications on a level tolerable for the group as a whole.

Yet another type of total situation is given in a staff support group composed of members some of whom work in different departments. The group starts with pre-existing sub-groups. In order to ensure the healthy survival and growth of the group as a whole, the group analyst will have to help the group again and again to become aware of its underlying structure and the implications for everyone in the here-and-now.

While no group analyst would want to set unrealistic boundaries, it is equally true that no group can function, or even exist, without boundaries. It is worth examining the rule of confidentiality in relation to staff support groups. Members who work together can hardly be expected not to discuss with each other topics that arise in the group. On the contrary—further debate on the same issues might be very useful. However, certain rules can be suggested: for instance, try not to discuss in sub-groups, and even less with others, what happened in the group. Instead, bring any unfinished business back to the next session. Another rule can run like this: Confidential or privileged information concerning patients or the work situation, and any personal facts disclosed in the group, have to remain within the group.

Where the group conductor has to be insistent and resilient is in protecting the boundaries of time and space of staff support groups. The total situation in which primary health care workers operate is characterized by constant time pressure exerted on them by patients, colleagues, administrators and an ever-increasing number of meetings of all kinds. The problem with time becomes apparent even before the group is formed. Discussions about when, how frequently, for how long and where to hold the planned staff support group involve a number of people. Whatever time is suggested, someone will point out that it is not possible. Finally, one of those present will cut through the maze of objections and make a decision.

It is not easy to carve out 90 minutes from a working day when the pressure is constantly on. However, there are differences, depending on the total working situation of group members. If the group consists of members of the same working team, the difficulty to attend punctually is very great at the start. It means that during the session their work comes to a halt: patients, colleagues, urgent paper work and so on have to wait. Members of the team might strongly resent the conductor who expects them to give such a high priority to their staff support group. After the initial difficulties, time-keeping becomes easy, and no one seems to remember what all the fuss was about. Even colleagues stop making amused and razor-sharp comments about the weekly 90-minutes' disappearance of the team. If members of the staff support group belong to different work teams, it may be more difficult to create a habit of weekly punctual attendance. Whenever a member has to finish work to go to attend the staff support group, he might be alone, without another colleague to help him resist the pressure to carry on working.

Another requirement is to find and keep a suitable room where the group can meet undisturbed. Objectively, this should not be too great a problem, were it not for the fact that the room is an attractive focus for acting out unconscious resistances against the staff support group and/or its conductor. For instance, the member of the group responsible for booking the room 'forgot' to do so this week and has not yet thought of making it a permanent booking. The member acts out his desire to have control over the group. Unconsciously and in a negative way he challenges the conductor's authority. If it were a therapy group, the conductor would do her best to bring such a dynamic to the group's consciousness and into the open. In a staff support group, where, unlike in a group-analytic therapy group, she has to relinquish the administration of some group boundaries to the members, she might have to be content if the group as a whole finds a practical answer to the 'room-booking problem'. In other words, it is good enough if the group as a whole counteracts on a reality level the unconscious destructiveness in its midst.

Unconscious attacks from all directions can threaten the group's survival. Colleagues and even senior staff who in principle approved the establishment of the group might unwittingly attack it. A moment before the session starts, a doctor catches one of the group members: 'Would you deal with this patient? It will only take you five minutes. Surely, your group will understand.' Another time there is a knock on the door. This has not happened for a long time. The key is turned anyway. The door remains closed, and the group carries on. Again a knock, then again and again. It goes on for at least ten minutes. Finally, despite the established rule not to open the door, someone in the group cannot stand it any longer, gets up and opens it. An equally nervous, deeply embarrassed and profusely apologetic clerk asks whether he can fetch some old papers from a cupboard. Investigations by members of the group after the session elicit the full facts: the first knocks were by the clerk's boss who, having seen how difficult it is to get access to the mysterious room, called him and ordered him to knock as long as necessary to fetch the papers.

Naturally, the group analyses such incidents and learns to understand better how and why other groups can unconsciously seek to undermine them in such a powerful way. The group as a whole might express its annoyance or talk about the event just for merriment's sake. In both cases the group analyst will watch out and prevent the group from sliding into destructiveness. Expressing anger towards others who are not present is not always helpful and can be destructive (Molnos, 1986). The useful question is, rather, what can we as a group do to communicate better with other groups and make them refrain from attacking us? The group analyst is responsible for how she conducts her group and to ensure its continuing and healthy existence. Part of this responsibility is to make sure that the group as a whole does not isolate itself from other groups but co-operates with others in an appropriate way.

Most of what has been said in this section could be repeated about staff support groups in other contexts. However, the difficulties described seem to be more numerous and more intense within HIV/AIDS programmes. This is true especially on the management level. All staff, including the managers working in HIV/AIDS-related programmes, are exposed to massive pressures, not only on a reality level, but also coming from the anxieties and unconscious impulses of many groups surrounding them. In addition, managers who are somewhat removed from the daily struggle experienced by staff caring for patients are convenient projection targets for split-off negative, even hateful, feelings coming from a number of groups. Objects of constant overt or unspoken attacks, the managers, would need support groups as much as or even more than others. It would be most desirable to set up staff support groups for managers as well or, where possible and appropriate, mixed groups of managers and other staff. However, since staff support groups can only survive with strong institutional backing, it will always be necessary that someone in a higher managerial position who is not a member of the same group protects and supports the conductor's work.

Staff in HIV/ARC/AIDS-related programmes often act as group conductors themselves. One of the main spin-offs of staff support groups conducted by group analysts is the experiential learning that enables its members to understand and handle group boundaries with confidence. It helps them to recognize the destructive forces in the here-and-now and to mobilize the group unconscious to constructive ends.

POSTSCRIPT

W hat is the conclusion? Is there a final conclusion to this book? None I can offer. The reader might find his own, personal one. If the preceding pages helped him to ease the anxiety about unacceptable impulses he had experienced against HIV-infected people, against those living with AIDS and dying from it, or against the carers who try to alleviate the distress of the latter, if he was made to think of coming to grips with age-old terrors by entering and using the magical space of a small group set up for the purpose of open exploration in an atmosphere of tolerance, mutual understanding and acceptance, this book has fulfilled its function.

The last thoughts turn to the dead and those who cared—to the thousands of patchwork quilts that lovingly cover myriads of treasured memories in the minds of those who designed and made them, those who remember. There are other losses as well. I think of the many exceptional people who work in this field and abandon it after a few years. I think of the health advisers who listen, day in and day out, sitting targets battered by waves of desperate human an-

175

guish, the first casualties of 'burn-out'. I think of Caroline and David who have gone to start new lives continents apart. They had given everything they could and then took with them all they knew, their caring nature, wisdom and vast experience. They left behind an indelible trace of love in the hearts of those who had worked with them.

The magical space . . .

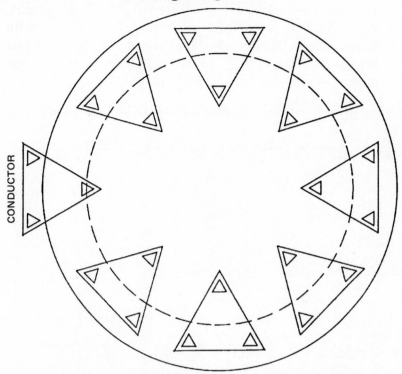

. . . of the small group conducted along group-analytic lines. The outer circle symbolizes the boundaries of time, space and conduct required that make the group safe and cohesive and protect it from others. Each of the eight triangles represents a person with his past history and current problems and joys, relationships and achievements, as well as his feelings and reactions in the here-and-now of the group session. The conductor sets aside her own past and current problems in order to focus on the group and guard its boundaries.

Figure 2.

This graphic representation of the group-analytic group, devised by the author, was first published in *Group Analysis, The Journal of Group Analytic Psychotherapy, 19* (1986), p. 213.

Leaflet

 **The Group-Analytic Society
and
The Institute of Group Analysis**

GROUP RESPONSES TO THE AIDS CRISIS
AN EXPERIENTIAL WORKSHOP

Saturday, 5th December 1987
9.30 a.m. to 4.45 p.m.

The aims of this workshop are:

(1) to explore group responses which occur in institutions and the community in relation to the spread of HIV/AIDS;

(2) to enable workers to become more aware of their own responses and deepen their understanding;

(3) to improve the ability of workers to contain the fear and the irrational reactions generated by contact with and around HIV/AIDS.

The workshop should be of interest to doctors, nurses, social workers, health advisers, counsellors, community workers, volunteers, their trainers, managers and administrators who are working in HIV/AIDS-related programmes.

Dr. Charles Farthing, MRCP, FRACP, Research Specialist in AIDS, St Stephen's Hospital, and Antony Grey, Convenor of the BAC AIDS-Panel will be among the speakers.

Experiential small groups conducted by qualified group analysts will give participants a chance to explore and express their own feelings.

Chairman: Malcolm Pines, FRCP, FRCPsych., DPM, past President of the International Association of Group Psychotherapy

Convenor: Angela Molnos, Ph D, Dip Psych, Group Analyst, assisted by Janet Boakes, MRCPsych, Group Analyst, Consultant Psychotherapist at St George's Hospital; and Dorothy M. Edwards, DPH, MRCPsych, Consultant Psychotherapist London Borough of Barnet, Social Services; Senior Registrar, Tavistock Clinic

Please apply early as numbers are limited.

Registration form

To: The Institute of Group Analysis, 1 Daleham Gardens,
London NW3 5BY

I shall attend the workshop 'Group Responses to the AIDS
Crisis' on 5th December 1987 and enclose a cheque for
£...... (made payable to 'The Institute of Group Analysis') in
payment of my fee.

Full Name: Age:

Address (including postal code):

Telephone:

Professional Background:

Are you in any way connected with activities or
programmes related to combating HIV/AIDS?

Yes/No (delete as appropriate)

If yes, please give details whether in primary care, administrative, managerial, training, etc. capacity, in what position, since when and where.

If no, can you say what attracts you to this workshop.

(We need this information to compose the experiential groups and to tailor the workshop to participants' needs)

Date: Signature:

Closing Date: 23rd November 1987

FEE: GAS/IGA
                   members   non-members
before 1.11.87:   £30.00   £35.00
after 1.11.87:   £35.00   £40.00

To include morning coffee, light lunch and afternoon tea.

Members of staff and speakers

JBa = Jim BAMBER, GAS, Highgate Counselling Centre (group conductor)

JB = Janet BOAKES, St George's Hospital (co-convenor)*

DE = Dorothy EDWARDS, Tavistock Clinic (co-convenor and group conductor)

CF = Charles FARTHING, St Stephen's Hospital (speaker)

JG = Jean GARNER, London School of Economics (group conductor)

AG = Antony GREY, Albany Society (speaker)

JH = John HEATLEY, Albany Trust (group conductor)

BL = Brenda LING, GAS/IGA (administrative director)*

AMh = Anne MHLONGO, IGA (group conductor)

AM = Angela MOLNOS, GAS (convenor and speaker)*

MP = Malcolm PINES, IGA (chairman and speaker)

CR = Cynthia ROGERS, YMCA (group conductor)

DV = David VINCENT, University College Hospital (group conductor)

*JB, AM were not in a small group.
BL organized and supervised the back-up services (secretarial, reception, catering etc.).

Group conductors' meeting

Saturday, 28th November 1987, 2 p.m.

Those expected to attend are:
Group Conductors (Jim Bamber, Jean Garner, John Heatley, Anne Mhlongo, Cynthia Rogers and David Vincent)
Administrative Director
Convenors (Janet Boakes, Dorothy M. Edwards and Angela Molnos)

AGENDA

1. Rationale behind the workshop, its aims and possible outcome

2. Who are the participants? (affilitation, knowledge, experience, motivation)

3. Programme: contents and timing (!!)

4. Composition of the small groups: selection criteria

5. Difficulties that can be anticipated in the groups:
   Hidden dimensions among members (e.g. someone lost
   a son; is HIV positive)
   What do we do with a manic AIDS worker (who
   provokes unspoken rage)?
   And with a member who goes suddenly pale, silent or
   even gets sick?
   And with the one who angrily obsesses about
   'uncaring' society, Govt., insurance people, GPs,
   dentists, the Catholic Church, etc., etc.?
   And with the one who obsesses about sexual practices?
   And with the anger exploding between group
   members?
   And with the AIDS 'bandwagon' or 'in-crowd' type?

6. Language: (a) Taboos (e.g. 'AIDS victims', 'high-risk
   groups'; 'homosexual'); (b) Terminological accuracy
   (e.g. distinction between HIV/ARC/AIDS)

7. 'Fishbowl' OR group reporting: aims and possibilities

8. Taking notes of events, impressions, observations, etc.
   in view of possible publication

9. Audio-tape all plenary sessions, talks and 'fishbowl'
   reporting

10. Karnac bookstall: any specific suggestions?

11. Administrative issues (i.e. which group in which room;
    what labels?)

12. Date of a follow-up meeting with those present and
    chairman.

13. Any other matters.

Programme for staff

*Eighth draft and FINAL programme revised in a meeting
with all group conductors and convenors on 28.11.87. For
staff use only. AM*

Saturday, 5th December, 1987
9.00 a.m. to 4.45 p.m.

The aims of this workshop are as follows:

(1)   to explore group responses and group phenomena
likely to be experienced by workers in institutions and the
community in relation to HIV infection and AIDS;

(2)   to enable workers to become more aware of group
phenomena and deepen their understanding of them;

(3)   to improve the ability of workers to contain the fear
and the irrational reactions generated by contact with and
around HIV/AIDS.

Chairman: Malcolm Pines, FRCP, FRCPsych., DPM, past President of the International Association of Group Psychotherapy

Convenor: Angela Molnos, Ph D, Dip Psych, Group Analyst, assisted by Janet Boakes, MRCPsych, Group Analyst, Consultant Psychotherapist at St George's Hospital; and Dorothy M. Edwards, DPH, MRCPsych, Consultant Psychotherapist London Borough of Barnet, Social Services; Senior Registrar, Tavistock Clinic

8.30–9.00   Group conductors + convenors + chairman meet in library

9.00–9.20   Arrival and registration (Coffee)

9.20–9.30   Opening words by the chairman, Malcolm Pines, and organizational announcements by Janet Boakes

9.30–9.50   Angela Molnos, Group-Analytic Society

Healing Power and Destructive Power of Groups
Group analysis and its relevance to the AIDS crisis—observations and personal experiences

9.50–10.20   Charles Farthing, MRCP, FRACP, Research Registrar in AIDS, St Stephen's Hospital

Reactions Within and Towards a Hospital's AIDS Team: observations and personal experiences

10.20–10.25 Questions from the floor

10.25–10.45 Antony Grey, Convenor of the BAC AIDS Panel, Chairman of the Albany Society

The Implications of the AIDS Crisis for Society at Large: observations and personal experiences concerning helpful and unhelpful responses within and between groups directly affected and other groups.

10.45–10.50   Questions from the floor

10.50–11.15   Coffee break

11.15–12.45   Small groups discuss the participants' own (and others') emotional reactions and group experiences related to the AIDS crisis. Group conductors will be especially aware of such phenomena as splitting, projection, and scapegoating in the here-and-now as well as in relation to the reported group experiences. Through the ideas presented in the talks all participants will be aware of the eight countertransference issues already identified in the USA among those who work with persons who are antibody positive or have developed ARC or AIDS, namely: (1) fear of the unknown, (2) fear of contagion, (3) fear of dying and of death, (4) denial of helplessness, (5) fear of homosexuality, (6) overidentification, (7) anger, (8) need for professional omnipotence.

Each group appoints a member (other than group conductor or chairman or speaker) to 'represent' it (see below)

12.45–1.45   Lunch

1.45–2.25   Group representatives (sitting in a circle in the middle of all others who just listen). A. Molnos acts as conductor. 'Reports' on what happened in the small groups. What experiences can be shared? Personal reactions to the workshop so far: what is missing? What are the needs for greater awareness of group phenomena and for group-analytic inputs related to the AIDS crisis? How can group analysts respond? Here-and-now reactions and experiences.

2.25–2.35　Break (to change chairs in rooms 2 and 3)

2.35–3.30　Small groups

3.30–4.00　Tea

4.00–4.30　Plenary discussion chaired by Malcolm Pines, co-chaired by Angela Molnos

4.30–4.45　Deliberations re. follow-up and conclusion

5.00–6.30　Wine in library with speakers, group conductors, convenors, chairman

The groups are:

David Vincent (downstairs, Room 3)
Anne Mhlongo (upstairs, Room 8)
John Heatley (upstairs, Room 7)
Jean Garner (downstairs, Room 4)
Dorothy Edwards (upstairs, Room 4)
Cynthia Rogers (downstairs, Room 2)
Jim Bamber (downstairs, Room 5)

Programme
for participants

9.00–9.20   Arrival and registration (Coffee)

9.20–9.30   Opening words by the Chairman, Malcolm Pines

9.30–9.50   Angela Molnos, Group-Analytic Society

Healing Power and Destructive Power of Groups: Group analysis and its relevance to the AIDS crisis—observations and personal experiences

9.50–10.20   Charles Farthing, MRCP, FRACP, Research Registrar in AIDS, St Stephen's Hospital

Reactions Within and Towards a Hospital's AIDS Team: observations and personal experiences

10.20–10.25 Questions from the floor

10.25–10.45   Antony Grey, Convenor of the BAC AIDS Panel, Chairman of the Albany Society

The Implications of the AIDS Crisis for Society at Large: observations and personal experiences concerning helpful and unhelpful responses within and between groups directly affected and other groups

10.45–10.50   Questions from the floor

10.50–11.15   Coffee break

11.15–12.45   Small groups

12.45–1.45   Lunch

1.45–2.25   Group representatives exchange experiences. A. Molnos acts as conductor.

2.25–2.35   10-minute break

2.35–3.35   Small groups

3.35–4.00   Tea

4.00–4.45   Plenary discussion (4.00–4.30)

Deliberations re follow-up and conclusion (4.30–4.45)

Evaluation form

This is to ask you to help us to evaluate the experiential workshop we had at Daleham Gardens on the 5th December. I would be most grateful if you could give your reactions on this sheet and return it in the envelope provided. The programme on the back of the page might assist you to recall the relevant points.

With anticipated thanks and best wishes for the New Year.

1. Was there any unexpected personal experience or particular observation you made during the workshop that you would like to share with us? If so, please describe it in some detail.

2. What aspects of the workshop did you find most useful/ pleasant/positive for yourself and what aspects less so?

3. Please indicate below if you have any further remarks to make on this workshop. We would also welcome suggestions and ideas for further HIV/AIDS-related workshops or seminars in the future.

REFERENCES AND BIBLIOGRAPHY

The references mainly cover the social and psychological aspects of the AIDS epidemic.

Acheson, D. (1988). *HIV-Infected Health Care Workers: Report of the Recommendations of the Expert Advisory Group on AIDS.* London: HMSO.

Alexander, F., & French, T. M. (1980). *Psychoanalytic Therapy: Principles and Application.* Lincoln, NE, & London: University of Nebraska Press (1st ed.: 1946).

Amchin, J., & Polan, H. J. (1986). A longitudinal account of staff adaptation to AIDS patients on a psychiatric unit. *Hospital and Community Psychiatry, 37* (12), 1235–1238.

American Psychologist (1988). *Psychology and AIDS, 43* (11: Special Issue).

Annales Medico-Psychologiques (1988). *AIDS and Psychiatry. 146* (3: Special Issue).

Batty, D. (ed.) (1987) *The Implications of AIDS for Children in Care.* London: British Agencies for Adoption and Fostering.

Beckham, D. (1988). Group work with people who have AIDS. *Journal of Psychosocial Oncology, 6* (1–2), 213–218.

196   REFERENCES AND BIBLIOGRAPHY

Bennett, F. J. (1987). AIDS as a social phenomenon. Tenth International Conference of the Social Sciences and Medicine (1987, Sitges, Spain). *Social Science and Medicine, 25* (6), 529–539.

Berg, B. L., & Berg, J. (1988). Aids in prison: the social construction of a reality. *International Journal of Offender Therapy & Comparative Criminology, 32* (1), 17–28.

Bohm, E. (1987). AIDS: Effects on psychotherapy in New York City. Special issue: AIDS: The psychosocial dimension. *Journal of Psychosocial Nursing and Mental Health Services, 25* (12), 26–31.

Bor, R., et al. (1988). AIDS counselling: Clinical application and development of services. *British Journal of Guidance and Counselling, 16* (1).

Bor, R., Perry, L., & Miller, R. (1989). A system approach to AIDS counselling. *Journal of Family Therapy, 11* (1), 77–86.

Boyd, K. M. (1987). The moral challenge of AIDS. *Journal of the Royal Society of Medicine, 80* (5), 281–283.

Brandt, A. M. (1986). AIDS: From social history to social policy. *Law, Medicine and Health Care, 14* (5–6), 231–242.

Buckingham, S. L. (1987). The HIV antibody test: Psychosocial issues. *Social Casework, 68* (7), 387–393.

Burgess, A. (1987). A plague on all our houses. *The Sunday Times Magazine,* June 21: Special Issue, pp. 10, 15.

Chodoff, P. (1987). Fear of AIDS. *Psychiatry, 50* (2), 184–191.

Christ, G., Beckham, D., Galo-Silver, L., & Shipton Levy, R. (1988). *The Role of Group Therapists in the AIDS Epidemic: Part B—Group Intervention Models for Persons with AIDS and Individuals Who Are HIV Positive.* Audiocassette Tape PW120-217AB, Forty-Fifth Annual Conference, American Group Psychotherapy Association, Inc. (25 East 21 Street, 6th Floor, New York, NY 10010), 1988 Group Psychotherapy Annual Meeting, February 8–12, 1988, New York, NY.

Cochran, S. D., & Mays, V. M. (1989). Women and AIDS-related concerns: Roles for psychologists in helping the worried well. *American Psychologist, 44* (3), 529–535.

Cohen, Stanley (1980). *Folk Devils and Moral Panics: The Creation of the Mods and Rockers.* Martin Robertson.

Cooper, A., & Bender, M. P. (1987). AIDS—What should psychologists be doing? *Bulletin of the British Psychological Society, 40,* 130–133.

Curran, L., McHugh, M., & Mooney, K. (1989). HIV counselling in prisons. *AIDS Care: Psychological and Socio-Medical Aspects of AIDS/HIV, 1* (1), 11–26.

Death Studies (1988). *AIDS: Principles, Practices, and Politics, 12* (5–6: Special Issue).

Dhooper, S. S., Royse, D. D., & Tran, T. V. (1987/8). Social work practitioners' attitudes towards AIDS victims. *Journal of Applied Social Sciences, 12* (1), 108–123.

Dickson, J. (1988). Crisis intervention in a situation of HIV infection. *Counselling. The Journal of the British Association for Counselling,* (64), 9–11.

Dunkel, J., & Hatfield, S. (1986). Countertransference issues in working with persons with AIDS. *Social Work (Albany, New York), 31* (2), 114–117.

Eisenberg, L. (1986). The genesis of fear: AIDS and the public's response to science. *Law, Medicine and Health Care, 14* (5-6), 243–249.

Ellens, J. H. (1987). AIDS: The pastor and patient–parishioner. *Journal of Psychology & Christianity, 6* (3), 19–24.

Essex, M., & Kanki, P. J. (1988). The origins of the AIDS-virus. *Scientific American, 259* (4), 44–51.

Evans, P. E. (1988). Minorities and AIDS. *Health Education Research, 3* (1), 113–115.

Fenton, T. W. (1987). Practical problems in the management of AIDS-related psychiatric disorder. *Journal Royal Society of Medicine, 80* (5), 271–274.

———— (1988). Psychiatric aspects of HIV infection: Implications for the UK. *Journal of the Royal College of Physicians (London), 22* (3), 145–148.

Finneberg, H. V. (1988). The social dimensions of AIDS. *Scientific American, 259* (4), 106–112.

Fluet, N. R., Holmes, G. R., & Gordon, L. C. (1980). Adolescent group psychotherapy: A modified fishbowl format. *Adolescence, 15* (57), 75–82.

Foulkes, E. (1979). Report on the Fourth European Symposium in Group Analysis, Stockholm, 26–28 August, 1978. *Group Analysis, 12* (1), 41–43.

Foulkes, S. H. (1948). *Introduction to Group-Analytic Psychotherapy: Studies in the Social Integration of Individuals and Groups.* London: Maresfield Library (1984).

———— (1964). *Therapeutic Group Analysis*. London: G. Allen & Unwin.

———— (1972). *Group-Analytic Psychotherapy*. Fort Lee, NJ: Behavioral Sciences Tape Library Sigma Information Inc.

———— (1975). *Group-Analytic Psychotherapy: Method and Principles*. London: Gordon & Breach.

Foulkes, S. H., & Anthony, E. J. (1957). *Group Psychotherapy: The Psychoanalytic Approach*. London: Maresfield Library (2nd edition: 1984).

Frierson, R. L., Lippmann, S. B., & Johnson, J. (1987a). AIDS: Psychosocial stresses on the family. *Psychosomatics, 28* (2), 65–68.

Frierson, R. L., Lippmann, S. B., & Johnson, J. (1987b). Psychologic implications of AIDS. *American Family Physician, 35* (3), 109–116.

Fuller, R. L., et al. (1988). Lovers of AIDS victims: A minority group experience. *Death Studies, 12* (1), 1–7.

Gallo, R. C., & Montagnier, L. (1988). AIDS in 1988. *Scientific American, 259* (4), 25–32.

Galy, N., et al. (1988). Human immunodeficiency virus infection among employees in an African hospital. *New England Journal of Medicine (Boston, MA), 319* (17), 1123–1127.

Gambe, R., & Getzel, G. S. (1989). Group work with gay men with AIDS. *Social Casework, 70* (3), 172–179.

Geis, S. B., & Fuller, R. L. (1985). The impact of the first gay AIDS patient on hospice staff. *Hospice Journal, 1* (3), 17–36.

Girardi, J. A., et al. (1988). Psychotherapist responsibility in notifying individuals at risk for exposure to HIV. *Journal of Sex Research, 25* (1), 1–27.

Gordin, F. M., et al. (1987). Knowledge of AIDS among hospital workers: behavioral correlates and consequences. *AIDS (London), 1* (3), 183–188.

Grant, D. (1988). Support groups for youth with the AIDS virus. *International Journal of Group Psychotherapy, 38* (2), 237–251.

Gray, L., & Harding, A. K. (1988). Confidentiality limits with clients who have the AIDS virus. *Journal of Counseling Development, 66* (5), 219–223.

Green, J. (1986). Counselling HTLV-III sero-positives. In: D. Miller et al. (eds.) *The Management of AIDS Patients* (pp. 151–168).

———— (1989). Counselling for HIV infection and AIDS: The past and future. *AIDS care: psychological and socio-medical aspects of AIDS/HIV, 1* (1), 5–10.

Green, J., & Miller, D. (1986). Hospital counselling: Structure and training. In: D. Miller et al. (Eds.) *The Management of Aids Patients* (pp. 187–193).

Greenblat, C. S., Katz, S., Gagnon, J. H., & Shannon, D. (1989). An innovative program of counseling family members and friends of seropositive hemophiliacs. *AIDS Care: Psychological and Socio-Medical Aspects of AIDS/HIV, 1* (1), 67–76.

Grey, A. (1987). AIDS: A counselling response. *Counselling. The Journal of the British Association for Counselling,* (59), 4–11.

Halter, Hans (1987). Das Virus muss nur noch fliegen lernen. *Der Spiegel,* No. 47, 240–253.

Hancock, G., & Carim, E. (1986). *AIDS: The deadly epidemic.* London: Victor Gollancz.

Harowski, K. J. (1987). The worried well: Maximizing coping in the face of AIDS. *Journal of Homosexuality, 14* (1–2), 299–306.

Hart, G. (1987). Placing children with AIDS. *Adoption and Fostering, 11* (1), 41–43.

Howe, E. G. (1988). Ethical aspects of military physicians treating servicepersons with HIV: III. The duty to protect third parties. *Military Medicine, 153* (3), 140–144.

Jacob, K. S., et al. (1987). AIDS-phobia. *British Journal of Psychiatry, 150,* 412–413.

Iglehart, J. K., & White, J. K. (1987). Policymakers grapple with AIDS costs and controversies. *Health-Progress (St. Louis), 68* (10), p. 18, 20, 23.

Isaacs, G. (1985). Crises psychotherapy with persons experiencing the AIDS related complex. *Crisis Intervention, 14* (4), 115–121.

Johnson, A. M., & Miller, D. (1988). Health care planning and social policy issues. *British Medical Bulletin, 4* (1), 203–219.

Johnson, J. M. (1988). AIDS-related psychosocial issues for the patient and physician. *Journal of the American Osteopathic Association, 88* (2), 234–238.

Journal of Psychosocial Nursing and Mental Health Services (1987). AIDS, 25 (12: Special issue).

Jung, C. G. (1961). *Memories, Dreams, Reflections.* Oxford University Press (Fontana Paperbacks) (1983).

Kain, C. D. (1988). To breach or not to breach: Is that the question? A response to Gray and Harding. *Journal of Counseling and Development, 66* (5), 224–225.

Karpman, S. B. (1968). Fairy tales and script drama analysis. *Transactional Analysis Bulletin, 7* (26), 39–44.

Katz, I., et al. (1987). Lay people's and health care personnel's perceptions of cancer, AIDS, cardiac, and diabetic patients. *Psychological Reports, 60* (2), 615–629.

Kermani, E. J., & Weiss, B. A. (1989). AIDS and confidentiality: Legal concept and its application in psychotherapy. *American Journal of Psychotherapy, 43* (1), 25–31.

Kim, C. R., & Rickman, L. S. (1988). Psychological aspects of the acquired immunodeficiency syndrome: A case report and review of the literature. *Military Medicine, 153* (12), 638–641.

Klein, S. J., & Fletcher, W. (1986). Gay grief: An examination of its uniqueness brought to light by the AIDS crisis. *Journal of Psychosocial Oncology, 4* (3), 15–25.

Koch, Michael G. (1987). *AIDS: vom Molekül zur Pandemie.* Heidelberg: Spektrum der Wissenschaft.

Krener, P. G. (1987). Impact of the diagnosis of AIDS on hospital care of an infant. *Clinical Pediatrics, 26* (1), 30–34.

Kübler-Ross, E. (1987). *AIDS: The Ultimate Challenge.* New York: Macmillan.

Lear, T. (1979). Post prandial reflections on the Fourth European Symposium in Group Analysis. *Group Analysis, 12* (1), 43–44.

Lessor, R. (1988). Fieldwork relationships on an AIDS ward: Verstehen methodology as a source of data. *Clinical Sociology Review, 6,* 101-112.

Lopez, D., & Getzel, G. S. (1987). Group work with teams of volunteers serving people with AIDS. *Social Work with Groups, 10* (4), 33–48.

McKusick, L. (1988). The impact of AIDS on practitioner and client. Notes for the therapeutic relationship. *American Psychologist, 43* (11), 935–940.

Magallon, D. T. (1987). Counseling patients with HIV infections. *Medical Aspects of Human Sexuality, 21* (6), 129–147.

Mantell, J. E., Schulman, L. C., Belmont, M. F., & Spivak, H. B. (1989). Social workers respond to the AIDS epidemic in an acute care hospital. *Health & Social Work, 14* (1), 41–51.

Marcus, R. (1988). Surveillance of health care workers exposed to blood from patients infected with the human immunodeficiency virus. *New England Journal of Medicine (Boston), 319* (17), 1118–1123.

Markova, I., & Wilkie, P. (1987). Representations, concepts and social change: The phenomenon of AIDS. *Journal for the Theory of Social Behaviour, 17* (4), 389–409.

Meisenhelder, J. B., & Lacharite, C. L. (1989). Fear of contagion: A stress response to acquired immunodeficiency syndrome. *Advances in Nursing Science, 11* (2), 29–38.

Melton, G. B., & Gray, J. N. (1988). Ethical dilemmas in AIDS research: Individual privacy and public health. *American Psychologist, 43* (1), 60–64.

Menz, R. L. (1987). Aiding those with AIDS: A mission for the church. *Journal of Psychology & Christianity, 6* (3), 5–18.

Miller, D. (1987a). HIV counselling: Some practical problems and issues. *Journal of the Royal Society of Medicine, 80* (5), 278–281.

———— (1987b). *Living with AIDS and HIV.* London: Macmillan.

Miller, D., Weber, J., & Green, J. (eds.) (1986). *The Management of AIDS Patients.* London: Macmillan Press.

Miller, R., & Bor, R. (1988). *AIDS: A Guide to Clinical Counselling.* London: Science Press.

Molnos, A. (1979). The self-healing small group. *Group Analysis, 12* (3), 192–195.

———— (1986). Anger that destroys and anger that heals: handling hostility in group analysis and in dynamic brief psychotherapy. *Group Analysis, 19,* 207–221.

———— (1987). El nosotros en el grupo analítico. In: José Agustín Ozámiz (ed.), *Psico-sociología de la salud mental* (pp. 47–61). San Sebastián (Spain): Ttartalo S.A.

Morgan, D. R., & Dawson, J. (1988). Occupational health aspects of the human immunodeficiency virus and AIDS. *Annals of Occupational Hygiene (Oxford), 32* (1), 69–82.

Murphy, D., Brown, L., & Primm, B. J. (1988). *Heterosexual Partners of IV Drug Abusers: Implications for the Next Spread of the AIDS Epidemic.* National Institute on Drug Abuse. Research Monograph Series, Mono 81.

Myers, W. A. (1987). Age, rage, and the fear of AIDS. *Journal of Geriatric Psychiatry, 20* (2), 125–140.

Nelson, M. O., & Jarratt, K. (1987). Spiritual and mental health care of persons with AIDS. *Individual Psychology. Journal of Adlerian Theory, Research and Practice, 43* (4), 479–489 (Special Issue: Pastoral counseling and the Adlerian perspective).

New Scientist (1987). Science of AIDS. *New Scientist, 113* (1553). Contributions by Jonathan Mann (AIDS in Africa), Michael Koch (The anatomy of the virus), Roy Anderson and Robert May (Plotting the spread of AIDS) and others.

Nichols, S. E. (1987). Emotional aspects of AIDS: Implications for care providers. Clinical Practice Issues in the Treatment of Drug Abuse and Addiction Conference. Number V: The AIDS epidemic 1986 (1986, Manhasset, New York). *Journal of Substance Abuse Treatment, 4* (3-4), 137–140.

O'Donnell, L. N., O'Donnell, C. R., Pleck, J. H., & Snarey, J. (1987). Psychosocial responses of hospital workers to acquired immune deficiency syndrome (AIDS). *Journal of Applied Social Psychology, 17* (3), 269–285.

Phillips, J. M. (1988). AIDS and ARC: pastoral issues in the hospital setting. *Journal of Religion & Health, 27* (2), 119–128.

Pitts, M., & Jackson, H. (1989). AIDS and the press: An analysis of the coverage of AIDS by Zimbabwe newspapers. *AIDS Care: Psychological and Socio-Medical Aspects of AIDS/HIV, 1* (1), 77–84.

Pleck, J. H., O'Donnell, L., O'Donnell, C., & Snarey, J. (1988). AIDS-phobia, contact with AIDS, and AIDS-related job stress in hospital workers. *Journal of Homosexuality, 15* (3–4), 41–54.

Posey, E. C. (1988). Confidentiality in an AIDS support group. *Journal of Counseling and Development, 66* (5), 226–227.

Richardson, D. (1987). *Women and the AIDS Crisis*. London: Pandora Press.

Rinella, V. J., & Dubin, W. R. (1988). The hidden victims of AIDS: Health care workers and families. *Psychiatric Hospital (Philadelphia Psychiatric Ctr, Pa, US), 19* (3), 115–120.

Ross, M. W. (1988). AIDS phobia: Report of 4 cases. *Psychopathology, 21* (1), 26–30.

Ryan, C. C. (1988). The social and clinical challenges of AIDS. *Smith College Studies in Social Work, 59* (1), 3–20.

Sabin, T. D. (1987). AIDS: The new 'great imitator'. *Journal of the American Geriatrics Society, 35* (5), 467–468.

Salt, H., Miller, R., Perry, L., & Bor, R. (1989). Paradoxical interventions in counselling for patients with an intractable AIDS worry. *AIDS Care: Psychological and Socio-Medical Aspects of AIDS/HIV, 1* (1), 39–44.

Schaffner, B. (1986). Reactions of medical personnel and intimates to persons with AIDS. Meeting of the American Academy of

Psychoanalysis (1984, New York, NY). *Psychotherapy Patient, 2* (4), 67–80.

Scientific American (1988). What science knows about AIDS. A single topic issue with contributions by R. C. Gallo, Jonathan Mann, Luc Montagnier, Jonathan N. Weber and many others. *Scientific American, 259* (4).

Shahoda, T., et al. (1986). AIDS: A time bomb at hospitals' door. *Hospitals (Chicago, IL)*, Jan. 5, 54–61.

Sherr, L. (1987). An evaluation of the UK government health education campaign on AIDS. *Psychology and Health, 1* (1), 61–72.

Shilts, R. (1987). *And the Band Played On: Politics, People and the AIDS Epidemic.* Penguin (1988).

Skeen, P., & Hodson, D. (1987). AIDS: What adults should know about AIDS (and shouldn't discuss with very young children). *Young Children, 42* (4), 65–71.

Sontag, S. (1978). *Illness as Metaphor.* Penguin Books (1983).

———— (1989). *AIDS and Its Metaphors.* Penguin Books.

Spector, I. C., & Conklin, R. (1987). AIDS group psychotherapy. *International Journal of Group Psychotherapy, 37* (3), 433–439.

Steel, M. (1988). IVth International AIDS Conference. *The Lancet,* July 2, 54–55.

Stevens, L. A., & Muskin, P. R. (1987). Techniques for reversing the failure of empathy towards AIDS patients. *Journal of the American Academy of Psychoanalysis, 15* (4), 539–551.

Sunday Times Magazine, The (1987). The AIDS-crisis. Special Issue. Contributions by Anthony Burgess; consultants: Michael Adler, Middlesex Hospital, London; Jonathan Weber, Institute of Cancer Research, London. *The Sunday Times Magazine,* June 21.

Swenson, R. M. (1988). Plagues, history, and AIDS. *The American Scholar, 57* (2), 183–200.

Temoskok, L., et al. (1987). The three-city comparison of the public's knowledge and attitudes about AIDS. *Psychology and Health, 1* (1), 43–60.

Turner, J. G., & Pryor, E. R. (1985). The AIDS epidemic: Risk containment for home health care providers. *Family and Community Health (Gaithersburg, MD), 3* (8), 25–37.

Valdiserri, R. O. (1988). The immediate challenge of health planning for AIDS: An organizational model. *Family and Community Health, 10* (4), 33–48.

Velimirovic, B. (1987). AIDS as a social phenomenon. Tenth International Conference of the Social Sciences and Medicine (1987, Sitges, Spain). *Social Science and Medicine, 25* (6), 541–552.

Vernon, R. G. (1988). The legal ramifications of AIDS in the workplace. *Psychiatric Hospital, 19* (3), 121–124.

Vollmoeller, W. (1988). Zum Thema AIDS in der Psychiatrie und Psychotherapie: spezielle psychodynamische und psychopathologische Aspekte anhand eines Falles mit 'AIDS-Phobie'. *Zeitschrift psychosomatischer Medizin und Psychoanalyse, 34* (4), 351–360.

Wagner, M., Fuller, D., & Nelson, D. (1988). *The role of group therapists in the AIDS epidemic: Part A—Training and desensitizing the professional.* Audiocassette Tape PW120-217AB, Forty-fifth Annual Conference, American Group Psychotherapy Association, Inc. (25 East 21 Street, 6th Floor, New York, NY 10010), 1988 Group Psychotherapy Annual Meeting, February 8–12, 1988, New York, NY.

Watney, S. (1987). *Policing Desire: Pornography, AIDS and the Media.* London: Methuen.

Weiss, S. H. (1988). Risk of human immunodeficiency virus (HIV-1) infection among laboratory workers. *Science (Washington), 239* (4835), 68–71.

Wertz, D. C., Sorenson, J. R., Liebling, L., Kessler, L. et al. (1988). Caring for persons with AIDS: Knowledge and attitudes of 1,047 health care workers attending AIDS Action Committee educational programs. *Journal of Primary Prevention, 8* (3), 109–124.

Widen, H. A. (1987). The risk of AIDS and the defense of disavowal: Dilemmas for the college psychotherapist. *Journal of American College Health, 35* (6), 268–273.

Wolf, J. (1988). Supporting HIV patients in the community. *Nursing Times (London), 84* (43), 75.

World Health Organization (WHO), Geneva (1988). *AIDS Prevention and Control: Invited Presentations and Papers from the World Summit of Ministers of Health on Programmes for AIDS Prevention.* Oxford: Pergamon.

INDEX

For concepts and issues relevant to the carers' work and to HIV/AIDS counselling, which do not appear in this index, or have only briefly been mentioned in the text—such as AIDS in prisons; children; elderly people; AIDS phobia; worried well; countertransference issues; economic, ethical, legal, policy making and political implications; consequences for community care; existential and religious questions; crisis intervention techniques; pastoral counselling—the reader is referred to the bibliography, pp. 195-204. Important authors like Adler, M., Bor, R., Fenton, T. W., Green, J., Hancock, G., Mann, J., Miller, D., Miller, R., Richardson, D., Sontag, S. and Weber, J. are among those listed in the bibliography, but not in this index.